MAX LUCADO

Curriculum Developed by
MICHAEL KELLEY

LifeWay Press®
Nashville, Tennessee

Published by LifeWay Press®
© 2010 Max Lucado
Second printing 2011

ISBN 978-1-4158-6878-2
Item 005271299

Dewey decimal classification: 248.84
Subject heading: CHRISTIAN LIFE

This book is a resource for credit in the Christian Growth Study Plan. For information, please visit www.lifeway.com/CGSP.

To order additional copies of this resource: write to LifeWay Church Resources Customer Service; One LifeWay Plaza; Nashville, TN 37234-0113; fax (615) 251-5933; phone toll free (800) 458-2772; order online at www.lifeway.com; e-mail orderentry@lifeway.com; or visit the LifeWay Christian Store serving you.

Printed in the United States of America

Leadership and Adult Publishing
LifeWay Church Resources
One LifeWay Plaza
Nashville, TN 37234-0175

CONTENTS

ABOUT THE AUTHOR

Since 1985, Max Lucado, has taken pen to paper, sharing his heart and his stories with readers around the globe. His books have been translated into more than 38 languages worldwide.

Max crafts memorable books for readers of all ages, races, and creeds. He has written best-selling books for both children and adults, from illustrated storybooks to nonfiction and biblical commentary.

Yet all these books and products find their wellspring in a single source: the pulpit at Oak Hills Church in San Antonio, Texas. All of Max's books for adults have been birthed as sermons for the congregation at Oak Hills Church, where he has served for 22 years.

Max Lucado is a minister who writes and a writer who preaches. He and Denalyn have three grown daughters—Jenna, Andrea and Sara, one son-in-law, Brett, and one sweet, but lazy golden retriever, Molly.

Michael Kelley is a writer, speaker, husband, and father from Nashville, Tennessee. Meet him online at *www.michaelkelleyministries.com*.

Dear Friend,

May I take just a moment to introduce you to a story that is very dear to my heart?

It's a story of hillbillies and simple folk, net casters and tax collectors. A story of a movement exploded like a just-opened fire hydrant out of Jerusalem and spilled into the ends of the earth: into the streets of Paris, the districts of Rome, and the ports of Athens, Istanbul, Shanghai, and Buenos Aires. A story so mighty, controversial, and head spinning that two millennia later a middle-aged, redheaded author from Texas would be writing a book that wonders:

Might it happen again?

This is the hope of this book, *Outlive Your Life*. Walking through the first 12 chapters of Acts, we see firsthand how a few faithful people can change the world. And we're asking, "Lord, do it again."

These are devastating times: 1.75 billion people are desperately poor, natural disasters are gouging entire nations, and economic uncertainty still reigns across the globe.

We are given a choice—an opportunity to make a big difference during a challenging time. What if we did? What if we rocked our world with hope? Will you join me in praying for a resurgence of compassion and outpouring of service? Will you ask God to do it again in this generation?

Let's hear it for the difference makers. I'm thanking God that you are one of them.

All the best,

Max Lucado

BEGINNING TO
OUTLIVE YOUR LIFE

Welcome to your six-week study of the Book of Acts, a story that will lead you to some principles to *Outlive Your Life*. Hopefully, this study is only the beginning of a journey of life-changing experiences through which you can have a lasting impact on the world. Here's how the study works.

At the beginning of each week, you'll get together with your Bible study group to view a video message from Max Lucado focusing on a key passage in the story of the Jerusalem church. Following the message, your group will be guided to respond to what you've heard.

During the next week, five daily readings and Bible studies will help you review that message, go deeper in your understanding, and then apply what you're learning to your daily life. Day 1 of each week starts with a chapter from the book, *Outlive Your Life* by Max Lucado. Days 2-5 will guide you through questions, activities, and Bible study designed by Michael Kelley to take you deeper into the key concepts of the week, integrating those principles into your personal life.

The Jerusalem church joined God's plan to change the world.

Let's get started doing the same ...

WEEK 1

OUR
ONCE-IN-
HISTORY
OPPORTUNITY

INTRODUCING OUTLIVE YOUR LIFE:

Welcome to your first small-group discussion of *Outlive Your Life*. It's going to be a great journey together, one in which you will discover the truths that motivated and empowered the first century world to be flipped upside down.

Introduce yourself to the group by sharing: (1) your name and brief information about your family; (2) where you spend most of your time during the week (home, school, business, etc.); and (3) why you chose to participate in this study.

This study's title is *Outlive Your Life*. What does that phrase mean to you?

Share with the group one person you have known personally who outlived their life. How did they do so?

Think about the following three questions:

1. Had you been a German Christian during World War II, would you have taken a stand against Hitler?

2. Had you lived during the Civil Rights movement in the South, would you have taken a stand against racism?

3. When your grandchildren discover that you lived in a day in which 3 billion people were desperately poor and 1 billion were hungry, how will they judge your response?

How would you like to be able to respond to the third question? How would you currently have to respond to that question?

VIEW DVD MESSAGE
"OUR ONCE-IN-HISTORY OPPORTUNITY"

You are the only chance the _____ has to experience what you have to bring.

There is something within you that makes you want to _____.

You want to live in such a way that the world will be glad _____ _____.

Ours is the _____ generation in the history of the church.

Ours is the most educated generation in the history of the church.

Ours is the _____ _____ generation in the history of the church.

Ours is the most technologically advanced generation in the history of the church.

Ours is the _____ _____ generation in the history of the church.

Two percent of the world's grain harvest, if shared and distributed, could eliminate hunger and malnutrition. There is enough food on the planet to provide every human being with a 2,500 calorie a day diet.

There are 132 million _____ worldwide.

There are over _____ million Christians in the United States alone.

If 6.49 percent of Americans adopted children, they could provide homes for every child orphaned by the AIDS epidemic.

The problem isn't the _____; the problem is in the _____.

This session is available for download at *www.lifeway.com/downloads*.

GROUP RESPONSE

What do you think it felt like to be part of the church in the time of the Book of Acts?

What do you think is the biggest obstacle to seeing things like those recorded in Acts happen today?

To which of these statistics presented in the video do you feel most personally connected? Why?

Do you agree with Max that the problem isn't in the supply but the distribution? Why or why not?

What is the responsibility of the Christian in light of both the supply and the demand?

What is the one thing you want people to say about you after you die?

Day 1

OUR ONCE-IN-HISTORY OPPORTUNITY

By the time you knew what to call it, you were neck deep in it. You'd toddler walked and talked, smelled crayons and swung bats, gurgled and giggled your way out of diapers and into childhood.

You'd noticed how guys aren't gals and dogs aren't cats and pizza sure beats spinach. And then, somewhere in the midst of it all, it hit you. At your grandpa's funeral perhaps. Maybe when you waved good-bye as your big brother left for the marines. You realized that these days are more than ice cream trips, homework, and pimples. This is called life. And this one is yours.

Complete with summers and songs and gray skies and tears, you have a life. Didn't request one, but you have one. A first day. A final day. And a few thousand in between. You've been given an honest-to-goodness human life.

You've been given your life. No one else has your version. You'll never bump into yourself on the sidewalk. You'll never meet anyone who has your exact blend of lineage, loves, and longings. Your life will never be lived by anyone else. You're not a jacket in an attic that can be recycled after you are gone.

And who pressed the accelerator? As soon as one day is lived, voilà, here comes another. The past has passed, and the good old days are exactly that: old days, the stuff of rearview mirrors and scrapbooks. Life is racing by, and if we aren't careful, you and I will look up, and our shot at it will have passed us by.

Some people don't bother with such thoughts. They grind through their days without lifting their eyes to look. They live and die and never ask why.

But you aren't numbered among them, or you wouldn't be holding a book entitled *Outlive Your Life*. It's not enough for you to do well. You want to do good. You want your life to matter. You want to live in such a way that the world will be glad you did.

But how can you? How can I? Can God use us?

I have one hundred and twenty answers to that question. One hundred and twenty residents of ancient Israel. They were the charter members of the Jerusalem church (Acts 1:15). Fishermen, some. Revenue reps, others. A former streetwalker and a converted revolutionary or two. They had no clout with Caesar, no friends at the temple headquarters. Truth be told, they had nothing more than this: a fire in the belly to change the world.

Thanks to Luke we know how they fared. He recorded their stories in the Book of Acts. Let's listen to it. That's right—listen to the Book of Acts. It cracks with the sounds of God's ever-expanding work. Press your ear against the pages, and hear God press into the corners and crevices of the world.

Hear sermons echo off the temple walls. Baptismal waters splashing, just-saved souls laughing. Hear the spoon scrape the bowl as yet another hungry mouth is fed.

Listen to the doors opening and walls collapsing. Doors to Antioch, Ethiopia, Corinth, and Rome. Doors into palaces, prisons, and Roman courts.

And walls. The ancient prejudice between Jew and Samaritan—down! The thick and spiked division between Jew and Gentile—crash! The partitions that quarantine male from female, landowner from pauper, master from slave, black African from Mediterranean Jew—God demolishes them all.

Acts announces, "God is afoot!"

Is He still? we wonder. Would God do with us what He did with His first followers?

Heaven knows we hope so. These are devastating times: 1.75 billion people are desperately poor,[1] 1 billion are hungry,[2] millions are trafficked in slavery, and pandemic diseases are gouging entire nations. Each year nearly 2 million children are exploited in the global commercial sex trade.[3] And in the five minutes it took you to read these pages, almost ninety children died of preventable diseases.[4] More than half of all Africans do not have access to modern health facilities. As a result, 10 million of them die each year from diarrhea, acute respiratory illness, malaria, and measles. Many of those deaths could be prevented by one shot.[5]

Yet in the midst of the wreckage, here we stand, the modern-day version of the Jerusalem church. You, me, and our one-of-a-kind lifetimes and once-in-history opportunity.

Ours is the wealthiest generation of Christians ever. We are bright, educated, and experienced. We can travel around the world in twenty-four hours or send a message in a millisecond. We have the most sophisticated research and medicines at the tips of our fingers. We have ample resources. A mere 2 percent of the world's grain harvest would be enough, if shared, to erase the problems of hunger and malnutrition around the world.[6] There is enough food on the planet to offer every person twenty-five hundred calories of sustenance a day.[7] We have enough food to feed the hungry.

And we have enough bedrooms to house the orphans. Here's the math. There are 145 million orphans worldwide.[8] Nearly 236 million people in the United States call themselves Christians.[9] From a purely statistical standpoint, American Christians by themselves have the wherewithal to house every orphan in the world.

Of course, many people are not in a position to do so. They are elderly, infirm, unemployed, or simply feel no call to adopt. Yet what if a small percentage of them did? Hmmm, let's say 6 percent. If so, we could provide loving homes for the more than 14.1 million children in sub-Saharan Africa who have been orphaned by the AIDS epidemic.[10] Among the noble causes of the church, how does that one sound? "American Christians Stand Up for AIDS Orphans." Wouldn't that headline be a welcome one?

I don't mean to oversimplify these terribly complicated questions. We can't just snap our fingers and expect the grain to flow across borders or governments to permit foreign adoptions. Policies stalemate the best of efforts. International relations are strained. Corrupt officials snag the systems. I get that.

But this much is clear: the storehouse is stocked. The problem is not in the supply; the problem is in the distribution. God has given this generation, our generation, everything we need to alter the course of human suffering.

A few years back, three questions rocked my world. They came from different people in the span of a month. Question 1: Had you been a German Christian during World War II, would you have taken a stand against Hitler? Question 2: Had you lived in the South during the civil rights conflict, would you have taken a stand against racism? Question 3: When your grandchildren discover you lived during a day in which 1.75 billion people were poor and 1 billion were hungry, how will they judge your response?

I didn't mind the first two questions. They were hypothetical. I'd like to think I would have taken a stand against Hitler and fought against racism. But those days are gone, and those choices were not mine. But the third question has kept me awake at night. I do live today; so do you. We are given a choice ... an opportunity to make a big difference during a difficult time. What if we did? What if we rocked the world with hope? Infiltrated all corners with God's love and life? What if we followed the example of the Jerusalem church? This tiny sect expanded into a world-changing force. We still drink from their wells and eat from their trees of faith. How did they do it? What can we learn from their priorities and passion?

Let's ponder their stories, found in the first twelve chapters of Acts. Let's examine each event through the lens of this prayer: Do it again, Jesus. Do it again. After all, "We are God's masterpiece. He has created us anew in Christ Jesus, so we can do the good things he planned for us long ago" (Eph. 2:10, NLT). We are created by a great God to do great works. He invites us to outlive our lives, not just in heaven but here on earth.

Here's a salute to a long life: goodness that outlives the grave, love that outlasts the final breath. May you live in such a way that your death is just the beginning of your life.

Max Lucado

"After David had done the will of God in his own generation, he died and was buried." **ACTS 13:36, NLT**

PRAYER

O Lord, what an amazing opportunity You have spread out before me—a chance to make a difference for You in a desperately hurting world. Help me to see the needs You want me to see, to react in a way that honors You, and to bless others by serving them gladly with practical expressions of Your love. Help me be Jesus' hands and feet, and through Your Spirit give me the strength and wisdom I need to fulfill Your plan for me in my own generation. In Jesus' name I pray, amen.

Excerpt from Outlive Your Life *(Nashville: Thomas Nelson, 2010), chapter 1.*

SUCCESS

Congratulations. You have been given the greatest gift in the universe: one human life. And you've only got one shot at it. But one shot at what exactly? To make money? To have a family? To excel at work and gain a little bit of power and prestige? Certainly that's how our culture encourages us, for it is by these marks that much of the world around us defines "successful living."

> **How do most people around you define *success*? What's your personal definition of *success*?**

> **How do you think God defines *success*? (Use Scripture passages or Bible stories to show God's definition.)**

Though only God knows for sure the specific plans He has for you in this world, we can all say certainly that God wants us to change the world.

> **How does that statement make you feel? Check the box applicable to you below.**
> ☐ **Excited**
> ☐ **Nervous**
> ☐ **Happy**
> ☐ **Skeptical**
> ☐ **Sad**
> ☐ **Other:**

Have you ever thought of yourself as a world-changer?
Why or why not?

It's a world that desperately needs changing. Consider again the startling statistics you encountered in yesterday's reading (pp. 12-13).

What images come to your mind as you read those statistics?
Does one of them stick out more than the others? Why?

What critical needs exist in the people of your own city?

Because these issues are so large and so complex, it's frankly much easier to ignore them. We wake up, eat a bowl of cereal, watch TV for a few minutes, and get in the car. And when we come home, we watch a little more TV, eat dinner, turn out the lights, and sleep well. We aren't bad people for living like that; we're not hurting anyone.

Then again, we aren't really doing anything to help either. The Jerusalem church had to face the immensity of the task before them, too. And just like us, they probably felt a little under qualified to so.

Read Acts 1:3;9-14. How were the believers different after the
40 days they spent with the post-resurrection Jesus?

Huge task. Small people. Similarly, here we stand in the midst of the wreckage of the world, the modern-day version of the Jerusalem church. But there is one word that can transform all our doubts into hopes. That word can alter our perspective from fear to expectation, from tragedy to opportunity. The word is *kairos*.

KAIROS

Its simple translation is "time." That doesn't seem like a perspective-changing concept at first, but let's keep digging. There are actually two Greek words translated as "time" into English. The first word is chronos. That word is used for ordinary measurements of time, as in "the time is 3 o'clock." But kairos is used in a different sense.

It's used to describe "the times." As in, when "the times reach their fulfillment" (see Gal. 4:4). Kairos is about a God-ordained, divine moment. This was such a time for the disciples. If we dig into the historical context of Acts, we see that the Lord had been working behind the scenes for quite some time to pave the way for what was about to happen.

Describe a situation when you experienced a kairos moment.

For the first time in human history, there was a network of roads connecting the major urban centers in the Roman Empire. Those roads were also guarded by Roman guard, for the world was in the middle of what was to be known as the Pax Romana, or the Roman Peace. One could travel to and fro throughout the empire without much threat of danger.

Also, a common language was spoken for the first time throughout the world, making communication easier and more efficient. People of all different races and cultures were, for the first time, moving into urban areas. Through these seemingly chance events, can you see the sovereign hand of God at work?

How did these factors set up the mission of the disciples?

What factors are occurring in our day that will allow for the church to make a greater difference in the world?

And here we stand, the modern-day version of the Jerusalem church. You, me, and our one-of-a-kind lifetimes and once-in-history opportunity. Is it too much of a stretch to believe that maybe God has been creating a kairos moment for us, too?

God has not given us these resources, this education, this money, and these abilities for no reason. He has not positioned us so favorably so that we might live well and pass money down to our children. The problem is not one of resources; the problem is one of willingness. And action.

The problems are great. So are the resources. But most importantly, so is the God we serve. Here we stand and the road is forked. The choice is one of inaction or action. So which will it be? What will we tell our kids?

We can respond with hope rather than despair. Optimism rather than defeat. Faith rather than doubt.

The task is big but so is the opportunity.

PRAYER

God of abundance, You have given richly to equip Your people for such a time as this. Thank you for the chance to live large lives. Help us to catch a world-changing vision of what we might be a part of in Your kingdom. In Jesus' name I pray, amen.

THE BAD NEWS

We are given a choice ... an opportunity to make a big difference during a difficult time. What if we did? What if we rocked the world with hope? Infiltrated all corners with God's love and life? What if we followed the example of the Jerusalem church?

They certainly didn't have the pedigree to be a world-changing force. At best, this rag-tag group was ordinary. At worst, well ...

And yet in the Book of Acts we find them taking the social issues, political systems, and spiritual lostness of the world by storm. We have no choice but to step back and wonder at the artistry of a God who can take the ordinary and make it extraordinary.

> **Read Ephesians 2:1-10. Make a list below of the adjectives Paul applied to his readers in verses 1-3.**

> **Which of those terms is most descriptive to you? Why?**

Dead. Disobedient. Children of wrath. That's not a great beginning to our story, but we've all been there. Crushed under the weight of condemnation. Face down in the sea of our own sinfulness. And if God, as the Master Artist, wanted to paint a picture of that situation, it would undoubtedly be the kind of painting that would stop you and make your mouth drop open. Lifeless eyes. Corpses. Darkness. No shades of bright colors representing hope. But then we come to Ephesians 2:4, and with two small words the picture morphs into something else.

"But God ..."

What a great expression! But God. There was hopelessness, but God ... There was death, but God ... There was darkness, but God ... Surely we can apply those same two words to so many instances in our own lives:

The cancer was advancing, but God ...
My son was wayward, but God ...
I was content to live for the best money could buy, but God ...
My marriage was in shambles, but God ...

What is your "but God" moment?

Can you remember the exact time God stepped into the equation? If so, when?

Was the change immediate or gradual? How so?

Everyone who has moved from Ephesians 2:1-3 to the rest of Ephesians 2 has had a "but God" moment. It's when, at the moment of deepest darkness, of most profound despair, of most inescapable hopelessness, God stepped into our lives and made us alive. Again.

Read Ephesians 2:4-10. How do the adjectives change after Ephesians 2:4?

If God were to paint the new picture based on these words, what would the painting look like?

That's our story in general terms. Death ... but God ... Life. But what then? We often think that's the end of the story; that once eternity is secure for us, once we have moved from being children of wrath to children of God, the picture of our lives is complete. But that great change, dramatic as it is, is not the end; it's the beginning.

Look back again at Ephesians 2:10 and see the Artist at work. The image of that verse is one of creativity. In other words, we are God's masterpiece. Much like an artist might step back and, with a great sense of accomplishment, look at the lines and squiggles that have come together to make up the work of his life, so God gazes in pride at His children.

It's been hard work, but He has steadily formed all our experiences, all our hopes, all our dreams, all our losses, and all our gains into one, dramatic picture. And it is beautiful. And unique! You are the masterpiece of the Divine Artist.

UTILITY

But here is the difference between God's masterpiece and those hanging in museums across the world: utility. Ultimately, any artist's masterpiece's utility is measured exclusively in beauty. That's what every painting, sculpture, or other artistic expression is for. It is meant for the purpose of beauty.

There is a similarity between God's masterpiece and all others in this fact. Surely no one can honestly gaze at the human body and not see beauty and creativity. We can't help but be in awe at the wonderful intricacies of human life. The same thing is true of people's stories. We can't help but be amazed at the way God weaves our experiences together to make us who we are. So in both of those senses, the purpose of God's workmanship is beauty. But there is another aspect, a different one, that separates both God as an Artist from other artists and us a creation from other masterpieces. Once again, the difference in found in Ephesians 2:10.

We weren't created to sit in a museum, to exclusively draw stares from those who admire our craftsmanship. We were crafted, created, and formed to do good works. And God has been preparing those good works ahead of time.

> **Are you more likely to live like your moment of salvation was the beginning or the end? Why?**

> **How does it make you feel to know that God planned works in advance for you to do?**

What types of things might stand in the way of you engaging in those good works?

How amazing. Much in the same way that God had been orchestrating events around the world to pave the way for the massive spread of the message of Jesus in the first century, He's been planning beforehand the good works for us in which we are to be involved. The plan of God is worldwide and individual; general and yet specialized; all-encompassing and yet unique.

These works are for you. Just you. It's true, you can't do it all, but God hasn't asked you to. He has, however, asked you to do what you are supposed to do. And you are meant to follow in the footsteps of the Jerusalem church. God is the Grand Orchestrator, the Master Painter. And He's got a wonderful plan for His masterpiece.

It's a plan for us to be useful, to be the changers of the world. And that plan takes into account everything that we are.

PRAYER

Creator, Former, and Redeemer, thank You for bringing life out of death. Please help us to see that we were created in Christ to do good works. May we grab on tightly to what You have for us to do in this life. In Jesus' name I pray, amen.

"You Shall Be Witnesses to Me ..."

"Do it again, Lord. Do it again ..."

That's the cry ringing in our ears as we look at how these ordinary people of the early church turned the world upside down. In the span of one generation, everything changed. These people went from the epitome of ordinary—the very definition of "everyday" and "common"—to leaders of a worldwide movement. As surprising as that is, it's exactly what Jesus said would happen.

Read Acts 1:8. What jumps out at you about the verse?

Was it a promise, a command, or both? What does that imply?

"You shall be witnesses to Me ..."

It's a command and a promise, a directive and a prophetic word all at the same time. It is at once an invitation and a prediction, and surely no one who heard Jesus say it fully grasped exactly how far it would go. Let's start with the first word: you.

Jesus' confidence in this verse is amazing. Looking out at who He was talking to, you wouldn't think He would brim with such gusto. Yet He did. There was no quaver in His voice, no hesitation in His statement. There was no "I hope" or "Maybe." Rather, in a note of absolute certitude, He smiled at the ordinary and told them that they would be extraordinary. *You shall.*

And it happened. They were. The very fact that you are reading these words is proof that they were. We are their legacy—living, breathing, reading testimonies that they indeed did. We are because they were.

Will we?

We're not fishermen. We didn't walk step for step with the Son of God. We aren't staring into the face of a Roman Empire. We didn't directly hear these words come out of Jesus' mouth. Nevertheless, we are part of the "you." The same statement Jesus made in Acts 1:8 applies to us. But do we really believe that it does?

How is Acts 1:8 applicable to your life?

What sorts of things might stand in the way of making that directive and promise the driving force in our lives?

Witnesses

We may not have walked in the footsteps of Jesus, but we nonetheless carry the mantle from Acts 1:8. Because we do, we too are "witnesses."

On the scale below, mark how favorably you react to the word witness.

Unfavorable   **Favorable**

Why did you answer the way you did?

Make a list of the top three things you think of when you hear the word witness.

1.

2.

3.

It's sort of an intimidating word, right? You might think of someone in protective custody because they know something they're not supposed to know. Or you might have a vision of a chair in the front of a courtroom where a person will sit to spill their guts about an accident or crime. Or maybe you thought of going door-to-door with gospel tracts, asking strangers about what they believe. Perhaps a guy on the corner wearing a sandwich board with the word "Repent!" painted on it flashed in your mind. It's no wonder we're content with being regular folks; being a witness is a big job with big implications.

I won't deny the bigness of the responsibility of being a witness. But I will say that perhaps it's a little simpler than we might think.

How would you define *witness*?

What do you have to know to be a witness? What do you have to do to be a witness?

A witness is someone who carries a piece of vital information because of something they have experienced. They have seen a car wreck and know who is at fault. They were privy to information and know where the trail of e-mails ends. They saw something, heard something, felt something, experienced something, and whatever that something is, is valuable.

That's it. No sandwich boards. No protective custody. Just the simple act of revealing what a person has experienced. That's what Jesus asked of His followers—what you have seen, heard, and experienced—you are to be witnesses of that.

Though there's always a verbal component to being a witness, there is also a tangible quality to it. Being a witness means caring for the sick. It means visiting those who have no one to visit them. It means bringing food to the hungry or rocking little babies in the neonatal unit of the hospital. It means preparing hot meals and singing carols at nursing homes. In all of these things, we are witnesses, because in all of those acts of grace and compassion we are bearing witness to what we ourselves have already received.

ORDINARY IS GOOD

And that's why being an ordinary Joe Pot Roast is actually good for us. Because we are so radically and unequivocally ordinary, there was absolutely no good reason for Jesus to do what He did for us. We are unimportant, misguided, and half-hearted. We are preoccupied and two-faced. But we are also something else: loved.

> **Read Romans 5:8. Using the space below, sketch out a brief timeline of the happenings recorded in this verse.**

> **What is significant about the "when" of Christ's death?**

He didn't wait for us to get our act together, to fully appreciate Him, or to completely understand exactly what was happening for us. While it might have looked different for all of us in certain ways, the universal truth for all Christians is this: While we had no hope and were absolutely lost, Christ died for us, not because we deserved it but because He loved us.

Because we are so ordinary and Christ died for us, we know what it's like for everyone else in the world who is ordinary. It is out of the extraordinary experience of ordinary people that we are witnesses. When we move out and testify as witnesses of the fact that Christ died for us, we bring hope to everyone in the whole wide world who is also ordinary.

In that sense, the very experience we have had with Jesus, whereby He invaded the ordinariness of our lives and graciously redeemed us, is what qualifies us to be witnesses. When we feed the hungry, clothe the naked, and verbally share the gospel, we are becoming extensions of the grace of God within us.

We are, in essence, just replaying in various forms and fashions what we have already experienced. As witnesses, we become conduits of the grace of God in our own lives. That's what it means to be true witnesses—those that live out what they have experienced. What they have seen. What they have felt.

> We become conduits, re-players of
> our own experiences with Jesus.

PRAYER

We all have a story to tell, Father. Help us to not only be faithful witnesses but excited ones. Impassioned ones. Vibrant ones. Help us to have the kind of excitement and passion that is infectious and contagious to a world in need. In Jesus' name I pray, amen.

YOU AREN'T IN IT ALONE

ALL OF YOU

If you look back at Acts 1:8 and consider the commissioning of the first church, it's striking to realize that although they were a group of individuals, Jesus didn't make individual assignments at that time. Remember His commission? "You [all of you collectively] will be my witnesses" (Acts 1:8, NIV).

We can only conclude that Jesus chooses to work in community.

Why do you think Jesus chooses to work in community?

Is that encouraging for you? Why or why not?

Changing the world is a group project. We are to corporately come together in the church with everything we have—all our talents, gifts, and resources—and team up to do something bigger with our lives.

You see the same emphasis, at least in part, in Jesus' prayer for His future disciples recorded in John 17.

UNITY ISN'T OPTIONAL

Jesus saw the need well before we did. In fact, our unity was so important to Jesus that He devoted time to it in His prayer the night before He died.

Read John 17:20-26. What specifically did Jesus pray in these verses?

Why do you think unity in the church is so essential for the world to believe in Jesus?

There in the garden, with His head beaded with drops of blood, Jesus approached the throne of His Father. And He prayed that His followers might be brought to complete unity.

Perhaps there is both a psychological and a practical reason for the vital nature of unity in the church. When you think about it, the gospel is much more than an invitation to heaven. It's a call to drastically and completely reorder your entire life. We are asking people to trust in a message that seems foolish. We are asking them to live their lives diametrically opposed to the culture around them. We are asking them to trust their entire lives, both in this world and the next, to a historical figure who we say was resurrected from the dead.

If we, in the church, are so drowned under backbiting and arguing, is there really any good reason for them to listen? If we can't agree amongst ourselves about what is truly important, why in the world would anyone listen to what we have to say about the most vital issues of life and death? When we come together in unity, we make a bold statement about the truth of the gospel to the world around us.

But there's a certain practicality to unity too. We've already discussed the magnitude of the task in front of us. We've delved into the immense and complicated problems of hunger, human trafficking, and spiritual lostness. We've looked these issues in the eye, and we've freely admitted that they are enormous. And we are small.

Unless we work together. What if Christians began to pool all their financial resources in order to eliminate poverty? What if we began to think strategically together about how to most effectively verbally share the gospel in areas of the world where Christ is not yet named? What if we put our homes on the line in order to welcome in the millions of orphaned children in the world?

We certainly can't do it alone. But together, the possibilities are endless.

What specifically do you think could be accomplished if the church decided to team up?

If so much more can be accomplished, why do you think Christians have such a hard time with unity?

What are three ways you might play a part in helping unify the body of Christ?

1.

2.

3.

In the light of the vastness of the mission, arguments and petty disagreements have a way of disappearing. Perhaps, then, the answer to the disunity we often find in the church is for the church to begin to ask itself, "What exactly are we here for?"

Are we really here to choose the color of carpet? Are we here to decide who has the most appropriate form of music? Are we here to endlessly debate the finer points of the gifts of the Holy Spirit?

Or are we here to change the world? Are we here to outlive our lives?

GROUP PROJECT

God wants us to outlive our lives, and He wants us to do it together.

Read Romans 12:1-10. Write out Paul's message in your own words.

What specifically do you think your specific role is?

What is God's will for your life? His will is that you play your essential role in the continuing mission of the church. That we come together in a group project and get busy about the work of His kingdom.

We're not all teachers. But the teachers should teach. We all don't have endless pocketbooks, but those who do should give. We all can't work to develop strategic plans, but those who can should. You don't have to do it all. But you do have to do something.

You don't have all it takes to complete the mission, and you're not supposed to. But you do have what you need to play your part in the massive group project of the kingdom of God.

The church cannot be who she's supposed to be until you are willing to be who you're supposed to be.

PRAYER

Creator God, thank You for forming and molding us as individuals. Help us not to think of ourselves more highly than we ought but to see ourselves as an integral part of the team of the church. May we give ourselves freely to each other for the greater good of Your mission. In Jesus' name I pray, amen.

OUTLIVING YOUR LIFE THIS WEEK

Scripture Memory: "After David had done the will of God in his own generation, he died and was buried" (Acts 13:36, NLT).

Action Plan: Schedule time with someone you admire who's making a difference. Ask these questions:
1. Why did you choose to live this way?
2. What motivates you?
3. What did you have to learn?
4. How did you begin?

WEEK 2

LET GOD UNSHELL YOU

GROUP REVIEW OF WEEK 1

What one truth sticks out from the study this week? What practical changes do you think God is calling you to make based on this week of study?

Look back at the Action Plan for week 1 on page 34. What was the most meaningful and impacting part of that activity for you? Why?

What was the moment when the shortness of life really hit home for you? Did your life change as a result of that realization? Why or why not?

Remember the portion of the study detailing Ephesians 2:1-10. What was your own "but God" moment?

What are some of the things that have happened in your life up to this point that have prepared you to participate in God's mission to change the world?

What does it mean to be called a "witness"?

What is your Jerusalem? Judea? Samaria? The ends of the earth? What are some specific ways you might be involved in being a witness to each of those areas?

VIEW DVD MESSAGE
"LET GOD UNSHELL YOU"

The Day of Pentecost

1. The _____ day of the year in Jerusalem
2. All men were expected to journey there at least once
3. Jerusalem swelled to one _____ people
4. Every element of humanity was represented there

This story is the earliest picture we have of the _____—right in the middle of a large city on the busiest day of the year.

> "Suddenly there came a sound from heaven, as of a rushing mighty wind, and it filled the whole house where they were sitting. Then there appeared to them divided tongues, as of fire, and one sat upon each of them. And they were all filled with the Holy Spirit and began to speak with other tongues, as the Spirit gave them utterance" (Acts 2:2-4).

The Holy Spirit comes as He _____.

> "They were all filled with the Holy Spirit and began to speak with other tongues, as the Spirit gave them utterance. And there were dwelling in Jerusalem Jews, devout men, from every nation under heaven. And when this sound occurred, the multitude came together, and were confused, because everyone heard them speak in his own language. Then they were all amazed and marveled, saying to one another, 'Look, are not all these who speak Galileans? And how is it that we hear, each in our own language in which we were born?' " (Acts 2:4-8).

An indoor prayer service became an outdoor _____.

God loves the _____.

God equips His disciples to declare His _____ in the languages of the peoples of the world.

Our job is to get in the middle of something and _____.

The promise of Pentecost is that if you are in Christ, then Christ's Spirit will equip you to speak the _____ of some people.

God has blessed you with a unique-to-you _____.

God gives _____ people an _____ ability to declare His wondrous works.

This session is available for download at *www.lifeway.com/downloads.*

GROUP RESPONSE

What are some ways we tend to shell ourselves off from the outside world? Why do you think we do that?

Describe what you might have seen on the day of Pentecost. What do you think the atmosphere felt like?

What's the significance of the Holy Spirit coming suddenly?

What are some of the implications of the day of Pentecost?

What's the significance of each person having a tongue rest on them as individuals?

What about you? What language do you speak most fluently? What in your life has led you to speak that language fluently?

Day 1
LET GOD UNSHELL YOU

May I show you my new clamshell? It just arrived. My old one was thinning out. You know how worn they can get. Sheer as the wall of a cheap motel. Mine was so chipped I could see right through it. And noise? It couldn't block the sound of a baby's whimper.

So I bought this new model. Special ordered. Tailor-made. Top-of-the-line. I can stand up in it. Sit down in it. Sleep in the thing if I want to. Go ahead, take a look inside. See the flip-down ledge on the left? Cup holder! Check out the headphones. As if the shell's insulation wasn't enough, I can turn up the music and tune out the world. All I do is step in, grab the handle on the interior of the upper shell, and pull it closed.

Better than body armor, thick as an army tank. Think of it as a bunker for the soul. In here the world has no hunger or orphans. And poverty? This shell comes factory coated with a sadness screen. Racism? Injustice? They bounce off my shell like rain off a turtle's back.

Let me tell you how good this baby is. I went to the convenience store this morning for coffee and a paper. I was standing in the checkout line, minding my own business, when I noticed the fellow in front of me was paying with food stamps. He wore a baseball cap, baggy khakis, and flip-flops and had three kids at his knees. Close enough to detect his thick accent, I pegged him as an immigrant. I can typically stir up a good smirk and pigeonhole these people as fast as you can say, "Burden on society." But this family started getting to me. The little girls were strawberry sweet, with their skin the color of milk chocolate and their almond-shaped eyes. One of them smiled in my direction. Before I knew it, I smiled back.

About that time the cashier shook her head and returned the food stamps. Apparently their value wasn't enough to cover the purchase. The father gave her a confused look. That's when it hit me. I can help him out. Little did I know, a cloud of kindness vapor had been released into the store. My body began to react. A lump formed in my throat. Moisture puddled in the corners of my eyes. I began to experience a sensation in my chest: gelatinous cardiacinus, better known as soft heart.

Then came the involuntary reflexes. My left hand lifted to signal my willingness. The other dug in my pocket for money. That's when I snapped to my senses and realized what was happening. I was under a compassion attack. I immediately lifted the lid of my shell and climbed in. I noticed other shoppers had already taken cover. I barely escaped. What would we have done without our clamshells?

Don't know what I'd do without mine. When news reports describe Afghan refugees, into the shell I go. When a homeless person appears with a cardboard sign, I just close the lid. When missionaries describe multitudes of lost, lonely souls, I climb in. Why, just last week someone told me about regions of the world that have no clean water. Without my clamshell to protect me, who knows what I would have done. I might have written a check!

This is quite a shield. You probably have your own. Most of us have learned to insulate ourselves against the hurt of the hurting. Haven't we? Mustn't we? After all, what can we do about the famine in Sudan, the plight of the unemployed, or a pandemic of malaria?

Clamshells. We come by them honestly. We don't intend to retreat from the world or stick our heads in a hole. We want to help. But the problems are immense (Did you say one billion are poor?), complex (When is helping actually hurting?), and intense (I have enough problems of my own).

That's true. We do have our own issues. Our sputtering marriages, fading ambitions, dwindling bank accounts, and stubborn hearts. How can we change the world when we can't even change our bad habits? We don't have what it takes to solve these problems. Best to climb in and shut the shell, right?

You would have had a hard time selling that strategy to the Jerusalem church. Not after God unshelled them on the day of Pentecost. Pentecost was the busiest day of the year in Jerusalem—one of three feast days that all Jewish men, at some point in their lifetimes, were required to appear in the city. They traveled from Europe, Asia, and Africa. It's difficult to know the population of ancient cities, but some suggest that during this season Jerusalem swelled from a hundred thousand to a million inhabitants.[1] Her narrow streets ran thick with people of all shades of skin, from Ethiopian ebony to Roman olive. A dozen dialects bounced off the stone walls, and the temple treasury overflowed with every coin and currency.

Then there were the locals. The butcher and his meat. The wool comber and his loom. The shoemaker, hammering sandals. The tailor, plying his needle. White-robed priests and unsightly beggars. Every element of humanity crammed within the three hundred acres of the City of David.[2]

And somewhere in their midst, Jesus' followers were gathered in prayer. "When the Day of Pentecost had fully come, they were all with one accord in one place" (Acts 2:1). This is the earliest appearance of the church. Consider where God placed His people. Not isolated in a desert or quarantined in a bunker. Not separated from society, but smack-dab in the center of it, in the heart of one of the largest cities at its busiest time. And then, once He had them where He needed them ...

> "Suddenly there came a sound from heaven, as of a rushing mighty wind, and it filled the whole house where they were sitting. Then there appeared to them divided tongues, as of fire, and one sat upon each of them. And they were all filled with the Holy Spirit and began to speak with other tongues, as the Spirit gave them utterance" (vv. 2-4).

The Holy Spirit came upon them suddenly—not predictably or expectedly or customarily but suddenly. Welcome to the world of Acts and the "sudden" Spirit of God, sovereign and free, never subordinate to timing or technique. He creates His own agenda, determines His own calendar, and keeps His own hours.

Fire and wind now. House shaking later. Visiting the Samaritans after water baptism. Falling on the Gentiles before water baptism. And here, roaring like a tornado through Jerusalem. "[The sound] filled the whole house" (v. 2) and spilled into the streets. The whistling, rushing, blowing sound of a wind.

The Spirit came, first as wind, then appeared as individual tongues of fire, "and one sat upon each of them" (v. 3). This wasn't one torch over the entire room but individual flames hovering above each person.

And then the most unexpected thing happened.

> "[They] began to speak with other tongues, as the Spirit gave them utterance.

> "And there were dwelling in Jerusalem Jews, devout men, from every nation under heaven. And when this sound occurred, the multitude came together, and were confused, because everyone heard them speak in his own language. Then they were all amazed and marveled, saying to one another, 'Look, are not all these who speak Galileans? And how is it that we hear, each in our own language in which we were born? Parthians and Medes and Elamites, those dwelling in Mesopotamia, Judea and Cappadocia, Pontus and Asia, Phrygia and Pamphylia, Egypt and the parts of Libya adjoining Cyrene, visitors from Rome, both Jews and proselytes, Cretans and Arabs—we hear them speaking in our own tongues the wonderful works of God.' So they were all amazed and perplexed, saying to one another, 'Whatever could this mean?' " (vv. 4-12).

Envision such a phenomenon. Imagine a cosmopolitan center such as New York City. Fifth Avenue is packed with businesspeople, laborers, and travelers from all over the world. Early one morning as the mobs throb their way to work, the sound of a wind shakes the boulevard. The roar is so stout and robust that people stop dead in their tracks as if expecting to see a train blaze down the avenue. Taxi and bus drivers brake. Silence falls on the city only to be interrupted by the voices of a group gathered in Central Park. One hundred and twenty people speak, each one standing beneath a different flame, each one proclaiming God's goodness in a different language. Witnesses hear their native tongues. José, from Spain, hears about God's mercy in Spanish. Mako, from Japan, hears a message in Japanese. The group from the Philippines discerns Tagalog. They hear different languages but one message: the wonders of God.

Oh to have heard this moment in Jerusalem. Andrew describing God's grace in Egyptian. Thomas explaining God's love to the Romans. Bartholomew quoting the Twenty-third Psalm to Cretans. John relating the resurrection story to the Cappadocians. Some in the crowd were cynical, accusing the disciples of early morning inebriation. But others were amazed and asked, "Whatever could this mean?" (v. 12).

Good question. Crowded city. Prayerful followers. Rushing wind and falling fire. Fifteen nations represented in one assembly. Disciples speaking like trained translators of the United Nations. Whatever could this mean?

At least this much: God loves the nations. He loves Iraqis. Somalians. Israelis. New Zealanders. Hondurans. He has a white-hot passion to harvest His children from every jungle, neighborhood, village, and slum. "All the earth shall be filled with the glory of the LORD" (Num. 14:21, ESV). During the days of Joshua, God brought His people into Canaan "so that all the peoples of the earth may know that the hand of the LORD is mighty" (Josh. 4:24, ESV). David commanded us to "sing to the LORD, all the earth! ... Declare his glory among the nations, his marvelous works among all the peoples!" (Ps. 96:1-3, ESV). God spoke to us through Isaiah: "I will make you as a light for the nations, that my salvation may reach to the end of the earth" (Isa. 49:6, ESV). His vision for the end of history includes "people for God from every tribe, language, people, and nation" (Rev. 5:9, NCV).

God longs to proclaim His greatness in all 6,909 languages that exist in the world today.[3] He loves subcultures: the gypsies of Turkey, the hippies of California, the cowboys and rednecks of West Texas. He has a heart for bikers and hikers, tree huggers and academics. Single moms. Gray-flanneled executives. He loves all people groups and equips us to be His voice. He commissions common Galileans, Nebraskans, Brazilians, and Koreans to speak the languages of the peoples of the world. He teaches us the vocabulary of distant lands, the dialect of the discouraged neighbor, the vernacular of the lonely heart, and the idiom of the young student. God outfits His followers to cross cultures and touch hearts.

Pentecost makes this promise: if you are in Christ, God's Spirit will speak through you.

Let God unshell you. And when He does, "make a careful exploration of who you are and the work you have been given, and then sink yourself into that" (Gal. 6:4, Message). Don't miss the opportunity to discover your language.

With whom do you feel most fluent? Teenagers? Drug addicts? The elderly? You may be tongue-tied around children but eloquent with executives. This is how God designed you. "God has given us different gifts for doing certain things well" (Rom. 12:6, NLT).

For whom do you feel most compassion? God doesn't burden us equally.[4] "The LORD looks from heaven; He sees all the sons of men … He fashions their hearts individually" (Ps. 33:13,15). When does your heart break and pulse race? When you spot the homeless? When you travel to the inner city? Or when you see the victims of sex trade in Cambodia? This was the tragedy that broke the hearts of three American women.

Ernstena is a pastor's wife. Clara is a businesswoman. Jo Anne had just started a small relief organization. They traveled to Cambodia to encourage Jim-Lo, a missionary friend. He led them to a section of his city where the modern sex trade runs rampant. An estimated fifteen thousand girls were on sale. At the time more than a hundred thousand young women in Cambodia had been sold into forced prostitution. Jo Anne, Clara, Ernstena, and Jim-Lo looked into the faces of teen girls, even preteens, and could see a devastating story in each. They began to snap pictures until the sellers threatened to take the camera away. The Christians had no idea what to do but pray.

The seedy avenue became their upper room. Lord, what do you want us to do? It's so overwhelming. They wept. God heard their prayer and gave them their tools. Upon returning to the United States, Jo Anne wrote an article about the experience, which prompted a reader to send a good deal of money. With this gift the women formed an anti-trafficking ministry of World Hope International* and provided housing for the young girls who were rescued or escaped from the brothels and sales stations. In just three years, four hundred children, ranging in age from two to fifteen, were rescued.

When the U.S. State Department sponsored an event called "The Salute to the 21st Century Abolitionists," they honored World Hope. They even asked one of the women to offer a prayer. The prayer that began on a Cambodian street continued in front of some of the most influential government officials in the world.[5] Amazing what happens when we get out of our shells.

"[God] comforts us in all our troubles so that we can comfort others. When they are troubled, we will be able to give them the same comfort God has given us." **2 CORINTHIANS 1:4, NLT**

PRAYER

Gracious Father, I am deeply grateful that You took the initiative to reach out to me—even in my sin and selfishness—in order to bring me into Your eternal kingdom, through the work of Christ. I cannot fathom such love! And yet, Father, I admit that too often I try to hoard Your grace, putting up walls of protection that I might keep hurt out and blessing in. I confess I am like the clam that shuts itself up in its shell, afraid of threats from the outside. Lord, I recognize that You call me to unshell myself and to partner with You in Your mission of love. Unshell me, Lord, so I, too, may reach out to a lonely, discouraged, and even hopeless world. In Jesus' name I pray, amen.

Excerpt from Outlive Your Life *(Nashville: Thomas Nelson, 2010), chapter 3.*

IN, BUT NOT OF

Pentecost was the coming out party for the Jerusalem church. They had been waiting and praying in the upper room, but then suddenly they were thrust into the public arena of Jerusalem on the busiest day of the year. God had literally brought the world to the doorstep of the church, and then He unshelled His followers into the midst of the international throng.

> **Read Acts 2:1-11. Make a list below of everything that happened as a result of the coming of the Holy Spirit.**

> **How did that occurrence relate to Jesus' commission recorded in Acts 1:8?**

But us? Well, it's pretty nice inside our clamshells. Away from any disturbances. Separated from needy people. Apart from anything uncomfortable. And let's be honest. We don't have what it takes to solve these problems. Better off with the clamshell since we can't do anything about those issues anyway.

> **What is the one, single issue in the world that is most difficult for you to ignore? Why that issue?**

What are some specific ways we try to insulate ourselves against the problems of the world?

Problem is that's not how Jesus taught us to live. He wanted His followers to be "out there," not "in here."

Read John 17:14-19. What do you think it means to be sent "into the world"?

What do you think it means to be "of the world"?

Where do you think we choose to spend most of our energies? Trying to not be of the world, or trying to be in the world?

SALT AND LIGHT

It's pretty cut and dried—Jesus wants His followers in the world. Not isolated. Not separated. In the midst, just as the church in Jerusalem was in the midst of the bustling city. To deconstruct the carefully formed clamshells of His followers, Jesus used some vivid imagery in His best-known sermon.

Read Matthew 5:13-16. Why do you think Jesus chose "salt" and "light" as metaphors for His followers?

What do you think it means to be "salt"? What about "light"?

Describe someone you know who embodies what it means to be salt and light.

You can say many things about salt. For example, in the first century salt was the primary means of preserving food. In a culture without refrigeration, salt was what kept meat from going bad. You can also argue that salt was, and is, what adds flavor to food. It makes food more palatable. It takes otherwise bland food and makes it erupt with flavor.

As for light, it's useful for showing the way. It chases darkness from a path or a room, giving you clear direction for what's ahead. Light brings comfort when there is fear; it brings truth about a situation that is otherwise indiscernible.

Though there are many applications as to how these metaphors relate to the Christians, both illustrations are built on this assumption: salt and light, in order to fulfill their purpose, must be uncontained. Salt does little good sitting in the shaker on the table. Light is not effective until the wick on the lantern is lit. Jesus was assuming in these illustrations that it would be the lifestyle of His followers to be out in their own Jerusalem, Judea, Samaria, and world, adding flavor to the blandness and dispelling the darkness around them.

Acts 2 is an example of light shining in darkness. They may have been nervous and apprehensive, but those early followers of Jesus felt something inside of them that could not be contained. It was as if the salt was begging to be poured out where it was needed. They responded by opening up their shells.

They found themselves interacting with people from all over the world. They were unshelled, and the world would never be the same.

I know it's comfy inside that shell. It's safe there. Familiar, too. But isn't there a part of you that wonders what it's like to be outside it? To be in the world? To be sent out? Let's see if we can feed that part. Let's leave the comfort, and when we do, we'll find that the outside, though challenging, is actually much better than the inside.

Outside the clamshell is where world-changers live. That's where you start to outlive your life.

PRAYER

You know our tendencies, God, to self-insulate. To self-protect. To hide. Would You, by the power of the Holy Spirit, break us out of our shells? Send us with power and love into those areas of our communities and world that are uncomfortable for us. In Jesus' name I pray, amen.

WAIT

Change the world. It's simple, but that doesn't mean it's simplistic. Nevertheless that's what Jesus told His followers to do. He gave them a God-sized mandate. Their mission included every country on earth. But strangely, before releasing them to accomplish it, He told them to wait: "Tarry in the city of Jerusalem" (see Acts 1:4). Now why would He give this instruction? This is a global assignment. Doesn't every minute matter? Every second count? Why would Jesus tell the followers to wait in Jerusalem?

So what about it? Why did they need to wait?

Using the scale below, rate your comfort with the Holy Spirit.

Uncomfortable   **Comfortable**

What has the interaction with the Holy Spirit been like in your own experience?

BIGGER-THAN-YOU POWER

Why did they need to wait? Simple. A "bigger-than-you" assignment demands a "bigger-than-you" power. Don't we need the same? We've been told to love neighbors who hate us, to forgive relatives who hurt us, to pray for enemies who abuse us, to send aid to countries who despise us, to love agnostics who mock us, and to go to a world that dismisses us.

Make a list of three words that come most readily to mind when you think of the Holy Spirit.

1.

2.

3.

Was "power" on your list? Why or why not?

Somewhere in Jerusalem, Jesus' followers gathered in prayer, waiting.

Read Acts 2:1-4. Notice the vivid language here. Why do you think Luke chose those particular words? What emotion was he trying to inspire in his readers?

The Holy Spirit came upon them suddenly—not predictably or expectedly but suddenly. Welcome to the world of Acts and the "sudden" Spirit of God, sovereign and free, never subordinate to timing or technique. He creates His own agenda, determines His own calendar, and keeps His own hours. But that's the nature of the Spirit. He's unpredictable. Maybe even a little dangerous. In fact, the literal translation of "the Spirit" is "divine wind" (see John 3:5-8).

How is the Holy Spirit like the wind?

In your experience, is there anything uncomfortable about following the Spirit?

Just as you can't control when and how the wind blows, the Holy Spirit blows as He sees fit. The Holy Spirit won't be dictated. He won't be contained. He's the embodiment of power, and power is what we need.

Read Ephesians 1:18-21. What three things did Paul pray for the Ephesian Christians?
1.

2.

3.

According to this passage, how great is the power in Christ followers? What is the evidence of that power?

This Holy Spirit, the same one invading the hearts of the early church, was the same Spirit at work when Christ was raised from the dead. That's astounding.

The Holy Spirit is more powerful than the most powerful of enemies. He's stronger than the strongest stronghold. He's more mighty than the unconquerable enemy. Every man has bowed under the weight of his own mortality, and yet the Holy Spirit remains strong enough to push back death. He did it in the case of Jesus Christ.

That's the Spirit at work inside us. The Spirit that was freely given at Pentecost. Imagine it: The Spirit who raised Christ from the dead is inside you and me. Ordinary people who have been made extraordinary by Christ in us.

If you had to pick one of the three options below, which would you say most characterizes your spiritual climate?

Mundane   Comfortable   Powerful

If we have this power at work inside us, then why do you think more Christians don't live powerful lives?

It's a valid question. Perhaps the answer is found in the difference between having and accessing power. We have been endued with what we need, in the Spirit, to complete the charge of Christ. But we also have an innate desire to stay where it's comfortable, cling to the familiar, and stick with what we know. To complete the mission requires a measure of faith on our part. We must believe that the Lord will tell us what to say, supply the courage we need, and fill us with the compassion we lack.

But the test of our faith is whether or not we actually act. When we act, we are putting our money where our mouth is, proving that we truly do believe the same Spirit that shakes houses, lights the tongues of men on fire, and raises the dead is indeed inside of us.

Time to let the Divine Wind blow.

PRAYER

What an amazing gift You have given to Your children! We confess our tragic unfamiliarity with the Holy Spirit. Help us to know and love the Spirit, recognizing the immense power You have given to us in Him for the working of Your purposes. In Jesus' name I pray, amen.

Day 4
DIFFERENT IS GOOD

IMAGINE THAT

Can you see the upper room of Acts 2 begin to shake in your mind? Here is the Holy Spirit, roaring like a tornado through Jerusalem. "[The sound] filled the whole house" (v. 2) and spilled into the streets. The whistling, rushing, blowing sound of a wind.

And the disciples found themselves able to speak in all kinds of languages and dialects, blessed with the sudden ability to articulate the wonders of God in the languages of the nations.

> Read Acts 2:4-13. What conclusions can you draw about the priorities of God based on this passage?

> What does the specific way the Spirit was manifested in the disciples tell you about God's plan and purpose?

Given the unusual circumstances, the people in the crowd responded with an appropriate question: Whatever could this mean?

> How would you have answered that question on the day of Pentecost?

What might this mean for us in the church today?

Pentecost means many things, but based on the specific gifting of the disciples, we must conclude that Acts 2 is about God's love for the nations. He wants His greatness to be proclaimed in every dialect under the sun.

CROSS-CULTURAL ENGAGEMENT

We shouldn't be surprised at this revelation. Cross-cultural engagement has always been a part of God's plan. Consider the very first missionary. We might be surprised to see that the mission endeavor didn't start in Acts. It started in Genesis. It started with Abraham.

In the space below, write the three things you consider most important to remember about the story of Abraham.

1.

2.

3.

Read the call for yourself in Genesis 12:1-3. What do you think would have been the most difficult part of the call for Abraham to believe?

Note the responsibilities of Abraham and what God promised to do in and through him in the space below.

Does the call of Abraham look familiar? We've seen it before. We saw it in the Great Commission. We saw it in Acts 1:8. The call is simple: "Go." It's the same call that remains on us. Go. Go out. Don't stay where you are. Go out from the comfortable to the uncomfortable. And don't just go a short ways— go all the way to the nations. And when you do, you will bless them with the greatest blessing available in the universe: the knowledge of God and the great message of Jesus Christ.

But to follow in the long line of Abraham, Jesus, and the Jerusalem church, we've got to embrace the Spirit of Pentecost. The Spirit that worked to put the wonders of God in the languages of the people. He's a culture-crossing God; we must be culture-crossing people.

If we open our eyes, we'd see that the nations have literally come to us. Refugees and immigrants are all around us, clustered in pockets inside our cities. The nations are within 20 driving minutes of most of us. All we have to do is open our doors, our eyes, and our shells and we will see men, women, and children of every ethnic descent already around us.

> **How many close relationships do you have with a person of a different ethnicity than your own? List them below.**

> **Is your list long or short? Why do you think that is?**

"And"

There is a key word in Acts 1:8 that, though small, is essential for us to understand and embrace. The word is "and." "You shall be witnesses to Me in Jerusalem, *and* in all Judea *and* Samaria, *and* to the end of the earth" (emphasis added). Not "or," but "and." Yet our distribution of resources reveals that we have an "or" versus "and" mentality. Take a look around inside most churches, and you'll find that the people sitting in the pews look remarkably similar to each other. Many of us might participate in a once-a-year effort to engage someone across the ocean, but when it comes to our daily lives, we are shockingly committed to being around people who look just like us. Only one problem—if we want to live the call of Acts, it's going to involve being around people who look, act, feel, and believe differently than we do. That's the "and" of Acts 1:8.

What is the biggest challenge of cross-cultural relationships for you?

What are some areas of your city or town where you would not likely be found? What are the people there like?

To outlive our lives, we must be willing to embrace the "and." To follow the Spirit to the nations. To the unfamiliar. To the different.

Better start getting out of our shells now because we've got eternity to spend with people who don't look like us.

PRAYER

God of the nations, You love the peoples of the world. We confess that many times we do not. Would You expand our vision to see the multiethnic, multicultural family of faith You are seeking? And help us to pursue that diversity with the same vigor You pursue it. In Jesus' name I pray, amen.

EACH

"What can this mean?" That was the question of the moment at Pentecost. Wind and power. Disciples becoming multilinguists. The wonders of God articulated. What do all these events mean?

They're about the power of God for salvation. They're about giving ourselves fully and completely to the mighty work of the Holy Spirit in and through us. But it should not be lost on us that Pentecost is also a tangible example of God's love for individuals.

Let's look again at what happened when the Holy Spirit came suddenly upon the first church. Though He came to them all, He came to rest upon each: "There appeared to them divided tongues, as of fire, and one sat upon each of them" (Acts 2:3). Each disciple was given a language. Peter didn't speak 15 idioms while the others listened. James and John weren't rewarded with multiple languages and others none. Matthias wasn't excluded for lack of experience. Each one had one. In fact, the number may have included the 120 followers. More than 12 languages were needed. More than 12 teachers were likely used. Mary, Susanna, the brothers of Jesus, and all the disciples were suddenly equipped to witness in a new way, each one having a unique voice.

Why is it significant that each disciple was given a tongue?

What principle concerning the manner of God's gifting can we learn from this situation?

Each and every person in the world speaks a different language. Even inside English, a worldwide language, there are different dialects. These individual expressions of language aren't so much learned in the classroom as they are through life experiences. God isn't just interested in communicating to people; He's committed to communicating to people in their heart language. He wants to speak to people in terms that are intensely personal to them.

THE WORD

Because every person speaks a different heart language, God is concerned about declaring His wonders in every one of those languages. To do so, He uniquely equips us, along with the Jerusalem church, to communicate His message. When He does, we find ourselves following the example of Jesus, who embodies this kind of communication.

Isn't it interesting that, of all the various names John could have chosen to describe Jesus in this first chapter of his Gospel, he centered on this: "the Word of God."

Read John 1:1-18. Why do you think Jesus is called "the Word"?

In a general sense, what purpose do words play in our lives? For what are they used?

Self-disclosure. That's what words are all about. There are certain things that can be observed about who you are just by looking at you. For example, a person might guess whether you work in a blue-collar or white-collar industry, your nation of origin, the way you choose to spend your money, and whether you had garlic for lunch just by being around you.

But to really know you—to find out the nitty-gritty details of your life, it requires speaking. Without words, a person will never know what makes you who you are. It is through the giving and receiving of words that we truly find out who someone else is.

Given that, we can say this: Jesus is God's final and ultimate communication to us of Himself. It is through Jesus that we know God. What makes Him happy and sad. What grieves Him and what makes Him excited. What He loves. Jesus is God's self-revelation to us in the language of humanity. In this, He is the Word of God.

OUR HEART LANGUAGE

The incarnation is about God reaching out to us in the most sympathetic way possible. It's about Him communicating the good news of the gospel in human terms. It's about the embodiment of all His compassion, goodness, grace, and mercy in our own language. Jesus, as the Word of God, teaches us the importance of meeting people exactly where they are. In their language.

> **Read Hebrews 4:14-16. What is the effect of the incarnation according to this passage?**

> **In light of Jesus' experiences as a human, how should we respond in our relationship with God? How about in our relationships with others?**

Because God chose to speak our heart language in the form of Christ, we never have to complain, "No one understands." God does, because He did. He knows physical and emotional pain. He knows what it is to be tempted. He knows the full range of human emotions and experiences because God chose, in Christ, to become one of us.

Because He did, we can always come to the throne of grace knowing we can find help. Understanding. Compassion. We find One there who speaks our language. And the biblical command is for us to follow Jesus' example.

Jesus said that as He was sent from the Father, He was sending out His disciples (see John 20:21). There is great truth in that single statement as we examine what it means to outlive our lives.

Read John 20:21. In what manner did the Father send Jesus?

What does that indicate about the way Jesus sends us?

You could say many things about the way in which Jesus was sent—He was sent humbly. Sacrificially. To Serve. But there is also this: Jesus was sent bodily.

God did not sit on His throne in heaven and shout declarations of His love and desire for relationship with His people. He didn't stay in the realm of glory. Rather, He got dirty. He got messy. As John said, the Word became flesh and dwelt among us (John 1:14).

Why is that fact significant?

What are some of the implications of God's willingness to come in bodily form to the earth?

That's how we are to go too. We are to go speaking the languages of the heart of the multitude of humanity that we come in contact with everyday. Similarly, at Pentecost, the disciples were sent out to speak the languages of the people. They weren't asking the crowds of international pilgrims to adapt to some other form of communication. No—God sent out His followers to meet people where they were. And connect with them in an intensely compassionate and understanding way.

God equips us to be His voice, to cross cultures and touch the hearts of people in their own language.

Our job? Well, our job is to get out of our shell. To start speaking the language He has given us. So what about you? What language do you speak? To what people group do you connect? The young? The old? The rich? The poor? The cancer patient? The single mother? They all have a dialect born of experience. And it's a dialect that you share.

Maybe it's time to start a conversation.

PRAYER

Word of God, thank You for allowing us to know You. Thank You for speaking the language of our hearts. Help us to do the same for others. Give us wisdom to see what language You have uniquely equipped us to speak. In Jesus' name I pray, amen.

OUTLIVING YOUR LIFE THIS WEEK:

Scripture Memory: "[God] comforts us in all our troubles so that we can comfort others. When they are troubled, we will be able to give them the same comfort God has given us" (2 Cor. 1:4, NLT).

Action Plan: Intentionally expose yourself to a variety of needs. Create a list of ways to get out of your comfort zone and listen to people in need. Make sure your schedule includes something in your neighborhood as well as something with international impact.

WEEK 3

DON'T FORGET THE BREAD

GROUP REVIEW OF WEEK 2

What one truth sticks out from the study this week? What practical changes do you think God is calling you to make based on this week of study?

Look back at the Action Plan for week 2 on page 62. What was the most meaningful and impacting part of that activity for you? Why?

Max inadvertently broke out of his clamshell with a family in line at the convenience store. When was the last time you had a compassion attack?

What are some of the ways we protect ourselves from such occasions, either implicitly or explicitly?

What are some of the ways we justify, whether legitimate or not, not helping people in need?

How does Pentecost demonstrate God's commitment to a multiethnic church? Why do you think it's so important to Him?

What's the biggest challenge in establishing cross-cultural relationships for you?

What would have to change in your life in order for you to come in more regular contact with people who are different than you?

VIEW DVD MESSAGE
"DON'T FORGET THE BREAD"

The first work of the church was an _____.

50 DAYS AGO:
Jesus was
_____

47 DAYS AGO:
Jesus rose from
the dead

10 DAYS AGO:
Disciples told
to _____
in Jerusalem

A FEW MINUTES AGO:
The Holy Spirit fell

NOW:
The ____·_____
of Pentecost

> "Men of Israel, hear these words: Jesus of Nazareth, a Man attested
> by God to you by miracles, wonders, and signs which God did
> through Him in your midst, as you yourselves also know—Him,
> being delivered by the determined purpose and foreknowledge
> of God, you have taken by lawless hands, have crucified, and
> put to death; whom God raised up, having loosed the pains of
> death, because it was not possible that He should be held by it"
> (Acts 2:22-24).

Who Is Jesus?

1. The miracles of Jesus are _____ of His divinity (v. 22).
2. Jesus is _____ of humanity's most important mission (v. 23).
3. _____ is no match for Him (v. 24).

The greatest defense of the resurrection is the _____ of Peter's
audience.

The question of the _____ became a question of the _____.

> "Repent and be baptized, every one of you, in the name of Jesus
> Christ for the forgiveness of your sins. And you will receive the
> gift of the Holy Spirit. The promise is for you and your children
> and for all who are far off—for all whom the Lord our God will
> call" (Acts 2:38-39, NIV).

God gives _____ to every person.

The first and foremost responsibility of the church is to declare God's _____ of our sins.

God offers second chances like a soup kitchen offers soup—to _____ who _____.

This session is available for download at *www.lifeway.com/downloads.*

GROUP RESPONSE

What were the essential elements of Peter's message?

Why do you think no one stood up to question Peter's explanation?

Why is the transition from "what does this mean" to "what shall we do" an essential one?

Are you more prone to focus on the spiritual healing or the physical meeting of people's needs? Why?

How does the gospel speak to both?

Why must we fully know and believe God's message ourselves in order to affect real change in the world?

Day 1

DON'T FORGET
THE BREAD

Denalyn called as I was driving home the other day. "Can you stop at the grocery store and pick up some bread?"

"Of course."

"Do I need to tell you where to find it?"

"Are you kidding? I was born with a bread-aisle tracking system."

"Just stay focused, Max."

She was nervous. Rightly so. I am the Exxon Valdez of grocery shopping. My mom once sent me to buy butter and milk; I bought buttermilk. I mistook a tube of hair cream for toothpaste. I thought the express aisle was a place to express your opinion. I am a charter member of the Clueless Husband Shopping Squad. I can relate to the fellow who came home from the grocery store with one carton of eggs, two sacks of flour, three boxes of cake mix, four sacks of sugar, and five cans of cake frosting. His wife looked at the sacks of groceries and lamented, "I never should have numbered the list."

So, knowing that Denalyn was counting on me, I parked the car at the market and entered the door. En route to the bread aisle, I spotted my favorite cereal, so I picked up a box, which made me wonder if we needed milk. I found a gallon in the dairy section. The cold milk stirred images of one of God's great gifts to humanity: Oreo® cookies. The heavenly banquet will consist of tables and tables of Oreo cookies and milk. We will spend eternity dipping and slurping our way through … OK, enough of that.

I grabbed a pack of cookies, which happened to occupy the same half of the store as barbecue potato chips. What a wonderful world this is—cookies and barbecue chips under the same roof! On the way to the checkout counter, I spotted some ice cream. Within a few minutes I'd filled the basket with every essential item for a happy and fulfilled life. I checked out and drove home.

Denalyn looked at my purchases, then at me. Can you guess her question? All together now: "Where's the bread?"

I went back to the grocery store.

I forgot the big item. The one thing I went to get. The one essential product. I forgot the bread.

Might we make the same mistake in a more critical arena? In an effort to do good, we can get distracted. We feed people. We encourage, heal, help, and serve. We address racial issues and poverty. Yet there is one duty we must fulfill. We can't forget the bread.

Peter didn't.

> "Now, listen to what I have to say about Jesus from Nazareth. God proved that he sent Jesus to you by having him work miracles, wonders, and signs. All of you know this. God had already planned and decided that Jesus would be handed over to you. So you took him and had evil men put him to death on a cross. But God set him free from death and raised him to life. Death could not hold him in its power" (Acts 2:22-24, CEV).

Peter was responding to the question of the people: "Whatever could this mean?" (2:12). The sound of rushing wind, the images of fire, the sudden linguistic skills of the disciples ... whatever could these occurrences mean? He positioned himself over the plaza full of people and proceeded to introduce the crowd to Jesus. Jerusalemites had surely heard of Jesus. He was the subject of a headline-grabbing trial and execution seven weeks before. But did they know Jesus? In rapid succession Peter fired a trio of God-given endorsements of Christ.

1. *"God proved that he sent Jesus to you by having him work miracles, wonders, and signs" (v. 22, CEV).*

Jesus' miracles were proof of His divinity. When He healed bodies and fed hungry bellies, when He commanded the waves as casually as a four-star general does the private, when He called life out of Lazarus's dead body and sight out of the blind man's eyes, these miracles were God's endorsement. God gave Jesus His seal of approval.

2. *Then God delivered Him to death. "[He] had already planned and decided that Jesus would be handed over to you. So you took him and had evil men put him to death on a cross" (v. 23, CEV).*

God deemed Christ worthy of God's most important mission—to serve as a sacrifice for humankind. Not just anyone could do this. How could a sinner die for sinners? Impossible. The Lamb of God had to be perfect, flawless, and sinless. When the Romans nailed Jesus to the cross, God was singling Him out as the only sinless being ever to walk the face of the earth, the only person qualified to bear "our sins in His own body" (1 Peter 2:24). The cross, a tool of shame, was actually a badge of honor, a badge bestowed one time, to one man, Jesus of Nazareth. But God did not leave Jesus in the tomb.

3. *"God set him free from death and raised him to life. Death could not hold him in its power" (Acts 2:24, CEV).*

Deep within the dark sepulchre of Joseph of Arimathea, behind the secured and sealed rock of the Romans, amid the sleeping corpses and silent graves of the Jews, God did His greatest work. He spoke to the dead body of His incarnate Son. With hell's demons and heaven's angels watching, He called on the Rose of Sharon to lift His head, the Lion of Judah to stretch His paws, the Bright and Morning Star to shine forth His light, the Alpha and Omega to be the beginning of life and the end of the grave. "God untied the death ropes and raised him up. Death was no match for him" (v. 24, Message).

I envision Peter pausing at this point in his sermon. I can hear words echo off the Jerusalem stones. "Death was no match for Him ... for Him ... for Him." Then for a few seconds, hushed quiet. Peter stops and searches the faces, his dark eyes defying someone to challenge his claim. A priest, a soldier, a cynic—someone, anyone, to question his words. "You are insane, Simon. Come, let me take you to Joseph of Arimathea's tomb. Let's roll back the stone and unwrap the decaying cadaver of Jesus and put an end to this nonsense once and for all."

What an opportunity for someone to destroy Christianity in its infancy! But no one defied Peter. No Pharisee objected. No soldier protested. No one spoke, because no one had the body. The word was out that the Word was out.

People began to realize their mistake. The gravity of their crime settled over them like a funeral dirge. God came into their world, and they killed Him. This was the thrust of Peter's sermon: "You killed God." "God proved ... to you ... All of you know this ... You took Him and had evil men put Him to death." You. You. You. On three occasions Peter pointed a verbal, if not physical, finger at the crowd.

The question of the hour changed. "Whatever could this mean?" (a question of the head) became "What shall we do?" (a question of the heart). "Men and brethren, what shall we do?" (v. 37).

They leaned in to hear Peter's reply. So much was at stake. What if he said, "It's too late"? Or "You had your chance"? Or "You should have listened the first time"?

Peter, surely with outstretched arms and tear-filled eyes, gave this invitation:

> "Turn back to God! Be baptized in the name of Jesus Christ, so that your sins will be forgiven. Then you will be given the Holy Spirit. This promise is for you and your children. It is for everyone our Lord God will choose, no matter where they live" (vv. 38-39, CEV).

Peter would eventually speak about poverty. The church would soon address the issues of widows, disease, and bigotry. But not yet. The first order of the church's first sermon was this: pardon for all our sins. Peter delivered the bread.

Would you allow me to do the same? Before we turn the next page in the story of Acts, would you consider the offer of Jesus? "I am the bread of life. Whoever comes to me will never be hungry again" (John 6:35, NLT).

The grain-to-bread process is a demanding one. The seed must be planted before it can grow. When the grain is ripe, it must be cut down and ground into flour. Before it can become bread, it must pass through the oven. Bread is the end result of planting, harvesting, and heating.

Jesus endured an identical process. He was born into this world. He was cut down, bruised, and beaten on the threshing floor of Calvary. He passed through the fire of God's wrath, for our sake. He "suffered because of others' sins, the Righteous One for the unrighteous ones. He went through it all—was put to death and then made alive—to bring us to God" (1 Peter 3:18, Message).

Bread of Life? Jesus lived up to the title. But an unopened loaf does a person no good. Have you received the bread? Have you received God's forgiveness?

We cherish pardon, don't we? I was thinking about pardon a few afternoons ago on a south Texas country road with hills and curves and turns and bends. I know it well. I now know the highway patrolman who oversees it.

And he now knows me. He looked at my driver's license. "Why is your name familiar to me? Aren't you a minister here in San Antonio?"

"Yes, sir."

"On your way to a funeral?"

"No."

"An emergency?"

"No."

"You were going awfully fast."

"I know."

"Tell you what I'm going to do. I'm going to give you a second chance."

I sighed. "Thank you. And thanks for giving me a sermon illustration on pardon."

God has posted His traffic signs everywhere we look. In the universe, in Scripture, even within our own hearts. Yet we persist in disregarding His directions. But God does not give us what we deserve. He has drenched His world in grace. It has no end. It knows no limits. It empowers this life and enables us to live the next. God offers second chances, like a soup kitchen offers meals to everyone who asks.

And that includes you. Make sure you receive the bread.

And once you do, pass it on. After all, if we don't, who will? Governments don't feed the soul. The secular relief house can give a bed, a meal, and valuable counsel. But we can give much more. Not just help for this life but hope for the next.

> "Turn back to God! Be baptized in the name of Jesus Christ, so that your sins will be forgiven. Then you will be given the Holy Spirit. This promise is for you and your children. It is for everyone our Lord God will choose, no matter where they live" (Acts 2:38-39, CEV).

So along with the cups of water, plates of food, and vials of medicine, let there be the message of sins forgiven and death defeated.

Remember the bread.

"For God was in Christ, reconciling the world to himself, no longer counting people's sins against them. And he gave us this wonderful message of reconciliation. So we are Christ's ambassadors; God is making his appeal through us. We speak for Christ when we plead, 'Come back to God!' For God made Christ, who never sinned, to be the offering for our sin, so that we could be made right with God through Christ." **2 CORINTHIANS 5:19-21, NLT**

PRAYER

My blessed Savior and Lord, I praise You for freely giving me the Bread of Life even though I deserved only the dust of death. In Your love You replaced my darkness with Your light, my fear with Your security, and my despair with Your hope. Remind me every day, Father, that the Bread of Life I have in Jesus comes to me by Your grace and through Your love—and that it delights Your generous heart when I tell others where they can find and partake of that same wonderful Bread. Make me, I pray, into an eager ambassador of Jesus Christ. Turn my fear into boldness so that heaven's streets may be filled with men and women who love the Savior, in part because they first heard of His grace and mercy from my lips. In Jesus' name I pray, amen.

Excerpt from **Outlive Your Life** *(Nashville: Thomas Nelson, 2010), chapter 5.*

"MEET JESUS"

Can you picture the scene in your mind? The people waited on bated breath. Some were cynical, sure, after the scene that had exploded before them. It had been a fairly normal morning, another year of the festival days. Then suddenly, out of nowhere, the group of people poured into the square speaking all kinds of languages. Bizarre. Strange. Even funny.

Some giggled and asked each other where the wine was that these men were obviously drinking. But others were intrigued: *What can this mean?* What can this message mean? What about the rumors? And what if they're actually true? What does all this add up to? Someone had to answer, and Peter rose to the occasion.

> **Read through Peter's sermon in Acts 2:14-40. If you had to point to a central truth and articulate it in one sentence, what would you say Peter's sermon was about?**

Peter took this opportunity—this flagship sermon of the Christian church— to succinctly articulate the centerpiece of the faith. He summarized it well in Acts 2:22-24.

> **Read Acts 2:22-24 again. What specifically did Peter say about Jesus?**

**Why do you think he chose these attributes of Jesus to
highlight to the crowd?**

JESUS IS QUALIFIED

*1. "God proved that he sent Jesus to you by having him work miracles,
wonders, and signs" (Acts 2:22, CEV).*

The mighty works of God in Christ weren't for a show. They were meant for
something more. Consider, for example, the very intentional way in which
John described these miracles in his Gospel. As you flip through its pages,
you see wonderful and amazing things happening. Wine coming from water.
Loaves and fish for thousands. Walking on the sea. And yet John chose to refer
to all of these occurrences not as miracles, not as wonders, but as "signs."

**Why do you think John chose that language to describe the
work of Jesus?**

In a basic sense, what is the purpose of a sign?

How do these works of Jesus fulfill that definition?

A sign, by its very nature, is meant to reveal or point to some previously
unknown piece of vital information. It might be a speed limit, falling rocks, or
a construction zone. In this case, all of the signs point to the God's absolute
and unconditional approval of Jesus. They are the endorsement of the Father

upon the Son. They are God's way of saying that Jesus is uniquely qualified to do what God had put Him on earth to do.

JESUS IS WORTHY

2. *Then God delivered Him to death. "[He] had already planned and decided that Jesus would be handed over to you. So you took him and had evil men put him to death on a cross" (Acts 2:23, CEV).*

We might balk in wonder at this. How could a God of love plan the murder of His one and only Son? Isn't that the very definition of cruelty? And yet upon further reflection, we see that these actions don't diminish but enhance our concept of the love of God.

> **Read Romans 5:6-8. Why do you think Paul felt it necessary to write that the cross was proof of God's love? Why is having that proof an important detail?**

The crucifixion didn't take God by surprise. He wasn't wringing His hands in worry, wishing He could do something to prevent it. He didn't slap His head and wonder how things got this out of control. It was at the appointed moment—at just the kairos-kind of time.

JESUS IS ALIVE

3. *"God set him free from death and raised him to life. Death could not hold him in its power" (Acts 2:24, CEV).*

> **How would the message of Christianity be different if Jesus hadn't risen from the dead?**

Read 1 Corinthians 15:17-19. What would the consequences be if Christ were not raised from the dead?

Death is the punishment for sin. It always has been, starting way back in the garden of Eden. And everyone has died. The coroner's report might have listed a heart attack, or drowning, or old age as the cause of death, but we know our sickness runs much deeper. Death is a reality because sin is a reality. But because Jesus rose from the dead, we know that death does not have to be our reality. Because of the resurrection, we have an everlasting hope that we, too, will follow His example. The resurrection proved Jesus' complete dominance, verified His claims about Himself, and provided a bedrock of unshakable hope for everyone on earth who believes in Him, for we all will face death someday.

Even today, the empty tomb is rock-solid proof. Every other religious leader that has ever lived and died is still where they lay, gathering dust and adding to the pile themselves. But Jesus? You can't point to the final resting place of Christ. You can't because He's not there.

And thus, the movement was born.

PRAYER

Lord of life and death, not even the grave could hold You down. You burst forth from the clutches of the greatest of enemies into life, and still today You lead a train of Your beloved people behind You. Thank You for the hope You have given to us. In Jesus' name I pray, amen.

TOO GOOD TO BE TRUE?

The true bread is the message of Jesus, and that's the message we must bring to the world. But why Jesus? At first glance, the simple message of forgiveness in Christ might seem to be a little too simple to throw at the immense problems facing the world today.

> **Make a list below of what you consider to be the three biggest problems facing the world today.**
> **1.**
>
> **2.**
>
> **3.**
>
> **What are the three biggest problems in your own community?**
> **1.**
>
> **2.**
>
> **3.**
>
> **Do you think there is a root cause to all those problems?**

Finding three (or 50) global concerns is no challenge. Stumbling economy. Polluted environment. Not enough water. Twenty percent of the world controlling 80 percent of its resources. Divorce, teen pregnancy, and drug abuse. Compiling a list of three problems is easy. Identifying the one that causes the others? Not as simple.

In a word, the problem is "sin." That is the source of every ill that plagues this race of humanity of ours. If that's the one big problem, then the one big solution is found in Jesus.

Peter confronted the crowd with the answer to their initial question of "What can this mean?" but then a strange thing started to happen. The gravity of their personal responsibility began to rain down uncomfortably on them.

> **Read Acts 2:36-37. How did the attitude of the crowd shift in these verses?**

> **Is personal responsibility an essential element to the gospel? Why or why not?**

Yes, it was God's plan. Yes, God was in control. Yes, God knew full well what was happening. No, that does not excuse you of personal guilt and responsibility. This was a fact that Paul, along with Peter, knew all too well.

No Excuses, No Exceptions

Remember Paul? Or should I say, remember Saul? That was his name before he had a face-to-face encounter with Jesus. That was his name when he was the violent pursuer, persecutor, and executioner of Christ followers. He was called Saul in dark houses of hiding Christians. He was called Saul by those who looked behind them as they walked to worship. He was called Saul by the early members of the Jerusalem church.

Paul knew a thing or two about being a sinner. Even the chief of sinners (see 1 Tim. 1:15). As such, he spent the first three chapters of his great letter to the Roman church discussing the universal problem and pervasive issue of sin.

Read Romans 1:18-23. As Paul says in verse 20, why are people "without excuse" before God?

What are some excuses people tend to make for their sin? Why do you think we are prone to make such excuses?

"I didn't hold the hammer."
"I never even met Jesus."
"I haven't done anything that bad."
"I'm not a murderer or anything like that."

The excuses could go on forever. We claim ignorance. We claim relative innocence. We claim a paltry bit of good works to our credit. But Romans 1 leaves no doubt—we are absolutely without excuse.

According to Paul, the very fact that humans live in the middle of creation makes us excuseless before God. Just by observing nature around us, there are certain things we know to be true about God. We know from observing the intricacy of the structure of an insect or leaf that God is creative. And careful. We learn from the coming and going of seasons, from the sunshine on a cool morning, and from the rain that refreshes the thirsty ground that God is kind and giving.

But instead of seeing these clues as pointers to the divine attributes of God, we have not been grateful. We have not been curious. We have not chosen to glorify Him. Instead, we have been prideful and boastful, taking advantage of God's good gifts without even so much as a thank you.

The bad news of Romans 1 is that from nature alone there is more than enough evidence of God to convict us. But from nature alone, there is not enough we can glean to save us.

Read Romans 3:10-18 and make a list below of the pronouns Paul used to describe humanity. What does his usage of those words indicate to you?

Do you think in today's culture it's becoming harder or easier for people to accept that they are sinners? Why or why not?

All. Not even one. No one. There is no room for exceptions in these verses. There are no exceptions for people who think of themselves as "not that bad." There are no free passes given for people who generally consider themselves good people. All are sinners. Absolutely. No exceptions.

We might try and deny it, but deep within ourselves we know it's true: we are sinners in great need. The crowd at Pentecost sensed it, and the question of the hour changed. "Whatever could this mean?" (a question of the head) became "What shall we do?" (a question of the heart). "Men and brethren, what shall we do?" (Acts 2:37).

What indeed? Peter had the answer.

PRAYER

Oh God, remind us today of our deep need for You. We are all sinners; we have all chosen evil over good, wickedness over righteousness. What shall we do? We have no hope apart from You. Intervene in us again, Father. Please. In Jesus' name I pray, amen.

WHAT SHALL WE DO?

Peter took his crowd through a myriad of emotions on the day of Pentecost. He began with a statement of the truth of the person of Jesus Christ. Then he moved to an element of personal responsibility for his hearers. It was in this moment that the question moved from the head to the heart. The crowd started by asking, "What can this mean?" Suddenly, they were asking, "What shall we do?"

> **Read Acts 2:38-39. What, according to this passage, did Peter advise the people to do?**

> **What do you think it means to "turn back to God"?**

Peter's message can be boiled down to this: believe and receive. Believe what he says about Jesus is true, and receive the forgiveness of a gracious God. Simple as that.

This is the way pardon for sins and eternal life is doled out—not to the best people but to the ones with open hands.

GOD'S OFFER

We are surely not the best people. Paul puts it well in Romans 3:23.

Read Romans 3:23. What do you think "the glory of God" is? In what way have we fallen short of it?

Why is falling short of God's glory linked with sin in this passage?

We must remember exactly why we were created in the first place. We weren't made because God was lonely. Or because He was bored. We were created to be mirrors of God's glory, to reflect the greatness of God in the world.

Ideally, as the image-bearers of God, we were meant to reflect back to God the thing of greatest worth and value in the universe: God Himself. But we have not. We have reflected greed. Pride. Anger. Lust. We have pursued life like we are the most important people in the world and have paid no mind to the glory of the One who created us. We have spurned the intent of our Creator. At a base level, that's what all sin is—it's a failure to recognize God as God.

We see that failure every time we lie, steal, or cheat. We see it in adulterous affairs. We see it in the stretched loopholes of tax returns. We see it in children who do not honor their parents. In all these things, there is a basic refusal to recognize the goodness and rightness of God and His ways. This is the one problem that prompts all others. We have dismissed God as king and made a play for His throne. We are mutineers on His ship, prodigals in His family. What Adam and Eve did first, we have done since. But God has made us a tremendous offer.

Read 1 Peter 3:18. According to the verse above, what is God's offer to humanity?

The rightful penalty for our sin is death. Both physical and spiritual death. We are personally responsible for the great and grievous consequences of sin, the consequences which extend to every person on earth. But Christ has suffered those consequences on our behalf. That is God's offer to you and me and "whosoever believes."

> **Read 2 Corinthians 15:17-21. Make a list below of what we receive, according to this passage, as a result of the work of Christ on the cross.**

> **What do you think it means to be "the righteousness of God"?**

> **Do you often think of yourself in these terms? Why or why not?**

> **How would truly believing that you are the righteousness of God change the way you live on a day-to-day basis?**

Unfathomable. Unthinkable. Incomprehensible. But it's true. At the cross, an exchange of epic proportions took place. Jesus Christ became sin for us. And we became the righteousness of God. He got our trespasses, our faults, and our sin, and we got His righteousness credited to our account.

This is the gospel. And it's true for all who are willing to believe. For the Asian. For the African. For the North American. For the hardened atheist and the church kid. Once for all. The gospel is true.

These are the facts of Calvary, and they are facts that reach past mere perception into the realm of faith and belief. Their truth extends beyond earth and into the farthest reaches of the cosmos. And that truth comes to you and me in the same fashion it came to those at Pentecost.

The answer is still the same for us as it was that day thousands of years ago. What shall we do? We should believe, and we should receive. We must believe Peter's message about Jesus, and then receive the outstretched arms of God. When we do, we'll find ourselves in the embrace of a loving Father longing to fill His house with children of every tribe, tongue, nation, and creed.

What about you? Have you received the Bread of Life?

If the answer is no, there's no time like the present. Open your heart and acknowledge the truth. That you are a sinner. That you want to be forgiven for those sins on the basis of Jesus' sacrifice. And that from this point on, you will live with Jesus as Lord.

Believe and receive.

PRAYER

You, O God, are both just and the One who justifies. You took the initiative when we fell so short. Thank You for so loving the world that You gave Your one and only Son for our salvation. And what a great salvation! We are eternally grateful. In Jesus' name I pray, amen.

PASS THE BREAD, PLEASE

THE TRUE BREAD

The crowd leaned in to hear from the bearded apostle. "What about it, Peter? What do we do with this message of Jesus?"

Three thousand people, hungry for forgiveness, took Peter at his word and were baptized. There must have been a great celebration in Jerusalem that day. It was a celebration centered on the Bread of Life.

Jesus once said, "I am the bread of life. Whoever comes to me will never be hungry again" (John 6:35, NLT).

But He didn't pull the statement out of the air. He spoke those words because of a specific incident that needed clarifying.

> **Scan through John 6:1-34. Make a list of the progression of events in this passage below.**

> **Given those events, what do you think Jesus was communicating by calling Himself the Bread of Life?**

In John 6, the crowd was almost overwhelming. But Jesus saw a grand teaching moment in the making. As such, He asked Philip a slightly rhetorical question: "Where shall we buy bread, that these may eat?" (John 6:5).

Jesus wasn't asking for caviar for the crowd; He was asking for bread. The basic staple of life. The simplest of meals. Yet it must have seemed like a silly request.

> **How did Philip respond to Jesus' question? What sort of attitude do you sense in his response?**

> **What would you have said if you were Philip?**

"Are you crazy?" Maybe that's part of what Philip wanted to say. He was no genius, but he could do this math. There certainly wasn't enough money in the treasury for a catering service—he didn't need to ask Judas to confirm that. Even if they had a couple years' average salary they couldn't feed the vast numbers before them.

But these people? These people looked like they hadn't had a decent meal in weeks. Surely they would eat more than the average person.

Fortunately, Andrew was eavesdropping. And though he didn't have a solution, he did have some information to contribute.

> **Recall John 6:1-14. Do you sense any difference in the attitudes of Philip and Andrew? What do you think was going through Andrew's mind when he offered up the loaves and fish?**

LOAVES AND FISH

There couldn't have been a more ordinary meal than the loaves and fish, but Jesus is in the business of taking the ordinary and making it into the extraordinary.

John 6 is one of those wonderful places in Scripture where we are left to imagine. Did all the loaves and fish appear at once? Did they gradually appear as the basket emptied? Were the disciples struggling under the weight of the multiplication of God? We don't know. What we do know is that Jesus didn't just provide; He abundantly provided. He provided so overwhelmingly that there were 12 baskets leftover. One for each of the disciples to carry as a reminder.

How do you think the crowd responded to the miracle?

What happened that night, according to John 6:16-21?

It was a busy couple of days for the Son of God. First the miracle of feeding at least five thousand people. Then walking on a raging sea. Then the reappearance of the massive crowd, which followed Him all the way to the other side of the lake.

The people followed Jesus, but their intentions weren't quite what Jesus wanted.

Focus on John 6:25-27. Why was the crowd following Jesus?

How did Jesus feel about that?

The sign of the feeding was great. It was proof of Jesus' power and His love. It showed both His ability and compassion. But His intention was something more. The people followed Jesus because of the promise of a free meal, but Jesus wanted to give them something more. Something better. Something eternally filling. Filling hungry bellies is good and right, but Jesus is not content to stop there. He wants to feed hungry souls.

THE PRIVILEGE OF DISTRIBUTION

There's another detail in this chapter that's worth pausing over. There were the disciples, their imaginations flip-flopping over what was before them. Loaves and fish coming from nowhere. Filling baskets. Overflowing baskets. And Jesus turned their way.

> **Read John 6:11. In this verse, with what did Jesus entrust the disciples?**

> **What principle can we learn from that?**

A generous boy. A miraculous touch. But the distribution? That was left to the disciples. The ones who had believed in the Bread of Life. The same thing is true today.

Jesus is still multiplying. Sure, He's multiplying water. Medicine. Money. But He's also multiplying grace. Mercy. Compassion. But He has given us, His followers, the privilege of distribution.

Read 2 Corinthians 5:19-21. What message has God given to His people? What are we meant to do with that message?

Once you begin to feast on the Bread
of Life, be sure to pass it on.

PRAYER

Father, thank You for entrusting us with the great joy and privilege of passing to the world what You have passed to us. Forgive us for neglecting this responsibility. Motivate us by Your grace, we pray, that we might be the distribution center for hope in the world. In Jesus' name I pray, amen.

OUTLIVING YOUR LIFE THIS WEEK

Scripture Memory: "God was in Christ, reconciling the world to himself, no longer counting people's sins against them. And he gave us this wonderful message of reconciliation. So we are Christ's ambassadors; God is making his appeal through us. We speak for Christ when we plead, 'Come back to God!' For God made Christ, who never sinned, to be the offering for our sin, so that we could be made right with God through Christ" (2 Cor. 5:19-21, NLT).

Action Plan: Pray for five friends, relatives, or acquaintances who you think may be far from God. For each of the five names, think of the next time you are likely to see that person. Pray specifically leading up to that anticipated meeting.

STAND UP
FOR THE
HAVE-NOTS

GROUP REVIEW OF WEEK 3

What one truth sticks out from the study this week? What practical changes do you think God is calling you to make based on this week of study?

Look back at the Action Plan for week 3 on page 90. What was the most meaningful and impacting part of that activity for you? Why?

How would you summarize Peter's Pentecost sermon in two sentences?

What are the key principles about the mission of God we learn from the day of Pentecost?

How do most people respond to the charge that they are sinners in need of a Savior?

What is the most effective way you've found to communicate this truth?

If we began to see Jesus as the true bread of heaven, how would that truth change the way we provide for people's physical needs?

VIEW DVD MESSAGE
"STAND UP FOR THE HAVE-NOTS"

> "As the believers rapidly multiplied, there were rumblings of discontent. The Greek-speaking believers complained about the Hebrew-speaking believers, saying that their widows were being discriminated against in the daily distribution of food" (Acts 6:1, NLT).

Jesus makes the _____ His priority.

"The acceptable year of the Lord" declares Jesus' radical commitment to the _____.

The Year of Jubilee was when God pressed the _____ button on the machinery of injustice.

The Year of Jubilee
1. All fields were allowed to _____.
2. All slaves were freed.
3. All property was returned to its original _____.

Jubilee guaranteed everyone an opportunity to get back on their feet.

God values a _____ _____ _____.

God never wants those who have a lot to be so far from those who have a little that they cannot _____ each other.

Twenty percent of the world's population enjoys an income that is _____ times the other 80 percent.

Seventy-five percent of the world's income goes to _____ percent of the world's population.

Why do some of us have so _____ when most of the world has so _____?

The first churchwide meeting in history was called to make the _____ our priority.

Scripture endorses Spirit-led _____ in which everybody does something.

"Poverty is _____ _____," Rich Stearns.

This session is available for download at *www.lifeway.com/downloads.*

GROUP RESPONSE

How was the problem of Acts 6 solved? What does the solution communicate about the priority of physical care for the poor? What does it communicate about spiritual care?

Why do you think Jesus chose the Scripture He did in Luke 4? What does that Scripture communicate about Him?

What do you think about the concept of Jubilee?

Why do you think God instituted it? Why do you think it was never practiced?

What do you think is the responsibility of the Christian in light of the uneven distribution of wealth across the world?

Day 1

STAND UP FOR THE HAVE-NOTS

Jim Wallis took some scissors to his Bible. He was a seminary student at Trinity Evangelical Divinity School when he and some classmates decided to eliminate a few verses. They performed surgery on all sixty-six books, beginning with Genesis and not stopping until Revelation. Each time a verse spoke to the topic of poverty, wealth, justice, or oppression, they cut it out. They wanted to see what a compassionless Bible looked like. By the time they finished, nearly two thousand verses lay on the floor, and a book of tattered pages remained.[1]

Cut concern for the poor out of the Bible, and you cut the heart out of it. God makes the poor His priority. When the hungry pray, He listens. When orphans cry, He sees. And when the widows in Jerusalem were neglected, He commissioned His best and brightest disciples to help them.

Rapid church growth brought needy people, and among the needy people were widows. They had no source of income. When they buried their husbands, they buried their financial security. Government support? Company pension? The Widows Job Corp? Didn't exist. According to the culture of their day, the extended family provided support. But extended families disowned Christian relatives, leaving the widows of the church with only one place to turn ... the church. The congregation responded with a daily distribution of food, clothing, and money.

That's when the trouble began.

> "But as the believers rapidly multiplied, there were rumblings of discontent. The Greek-speaking believers complained about the Hebrew-speaking believers, saying that their widows were being discriminated against in the daily distribution of food" (Acts 6:1, NLT).

The Greek-speaking widows were overlooked. Why? They were outsiders. Immigrants. These women didn't grow up in Judea or Galilee. They hailed from the distant lands of Greece, Rome, and Syria. If they spoke Aramaic at all, they did so with an accent.

Consequently, they were "neglected in the daily distribution" (NKJV). The driver of the Meals on Wheels® truck skipped their houses. The manager of the food pantry permitted Hebrew women the first pick. The food bank director separated requests into two stacks: locals and immigrants.

How did the church respond? I'm picturing a called meeting of the apostles, a circle of bearded faces: Andrew, John, Peter, Thomas, and the others. They heard the concerns of the women and pondered their options. They could dismiss them entirely. They could ignore the needy, neglect the neglected. After all, the apostles were spiritual leaders. They fed souls, not stomachs. They dealt in matters of sin and salvation, not sandals and soup. Couldn't they dismiss the disparity as an unnecessary concern? They could, except for one problem. Their Master didn't.

Jesus, in His first message, declared His passion for the poor. Early in His ministry He returned to His hometown of Nazareth to deliver an inaugural address of sorts. He entered the same synagogue where He had worshiped as a young man and looked into the faces of the villagers. They were simple folk: stonecutters, carpenters, and craftsmen. They survived on minimal wages and lived beneath the shadow of Roman oppression. There wasn't much good news in Nazareth.

But this day was special. Jesus was in town. The hometown boy who had made the big time. They asked Him to read Scripture, and He accepted. "And He was handed the book of the prophet Isaiah. And when He had opened the book, He found the place where it was written" (Luke 4:17).

This is the only such moment in all the Gospels. Jesus quoted Scripture many times. But the Son of God selecting and reading Scripture? This is it. On the singular occasion we know of, which verse did He choose? He shuffled the scroll toward the end of the text and read, "The Spirit of the Lord is upon Me, because He has anointed Me to preach the gospel to the poor; He has sent Me to heal the brokenhearted" (Luke 4:18, quoting Isaiah 61:1).

Jesus lifted His eyes from the parchment and quoted the rest of the words. The crowd, who cherished the words as much as He did, mouthed the lines along with Him. "To proclaim liberty to the captives and recovery of sight to the blind, to set at liberty those who are oppressed; to proclaim the acceptable year of the Lord" (Luke 4:18-19).

Jesus had a target audience. The poor. The brokenhearted. Captives. The blind and oppressed.

His to-do list? Help for the body and soul, strength for the physical and the spiritual, therapy for the temporal and eternal. "This is my mission statement," Jesus declared. The Nazareth Manifesto.

Preach the gospel to the poor.
Heal the brokenhearted.
Proclaim liberty to the captives.
Proclaim recovery of sight to the blind.
Set at liberty those who are oppressed.
And proclaim the acceptable year of the Lord.

"Acceptable year of the Lord" describes, perhaps more than any other words, Jesus' radical commitment to the poor. They are reminiscent of the year of Jubilee, a twice-in-a-century celebration intended to press the restart button on the machinery of justice.[2] Beginning on the Day of Atonement, all the fields were allowed to rest. No farming permitted. The fallow land could recover from forty-nine years of planting and harvesting.

In addition, all the slaves were freed. Anyone who had been sold into slavery or who had sold himself into slavery to pay off debt was released. Bondage ended.

And as if the soil sabbatical and slave emancipation weren't enough, all property was returned to its original owners. In the agricultural society, land was capital. Families could lose their land through calamity, sickness, or even laziness. The Jubilee provision guaranteed that every family, at least twice a century, would have the opportunity to get back on its feet.

Consider the impact of this Jubilee decree. A drought destroys a farmer's crop and leaves the family impoverished. In order to survive, the farmer decides to sell his property and hire out as a day laborer. A sharp investor swoops into the region and buys the farm and also a neighbor's. Within short order the developer has a monopoly, and the farmer has nothing but a prayer.

But then comes the year of Jubilee, what one scholar described as a "regularly scheduled revolution."[3] God shakes the social Etch A Sketch®, and everyone is given a clean slate. This injunction was intended to prevent a permanent underclass of poverty and slavery. People could still be rich, very rich, but they could not build their wealth on the backs of the very poor.

As far as we know, the people of Israel never practiced the year of Jubilee. Still, Jesus alluded to it in His inaugural address. What does this say about God's heart? At least this: He values a level playing field. In His society the Have-a-Lots and the Have-a-Littles are never to be so far apart that they can't see each other. Can they see each other today?

Not very well. According to a United Nations Human Development Report, three quarters of the world's income goes to 20 percent of the world's population.[4] Statistics can stagnate, so try this word picture.

Ten dairy farmers occupy the same valley. Among them, they own ten milk cows. But the cows aren't evenly distributed among the ten farmers—not one cow to one farmer. It's more like this: two of the farmers own eight cows, and the other eight farmers share two cows. Does that seem fair?

The two of us who own the eight cows might say, "I worked for my cows." Or "It's not my fault that we have more cows." Perhaps we should try this question: Why do a few of us have so much and most of us have so little?

I spent the better part of a morning pondering such a question on the Ethiopian farm of Dadhi. Dadhi is a sturdy but struggling husband and father. His dirt-floored mud hut would fit easily in my garage. His wife's handwoven baskets decorate his walls. Straw mats are rolled and stored against the sides, awaiting nightfall when all seven family members will sleep on them. Dadhi's five children smile quickly and hug tightly. They don't know how poor they are.

Dadhi does. He earns less than a dollar a day at a nearby farm. He'd work his own land, except a plague took the life of his ox. His only one. With no ox, he can't plow. With no plowed field, he can't sow a crop. If he can't sow a crop, he can't harvest one. All he needs is an ox.

Dadhi is energetic and industrious. He has mastered a trade and been faithful to his wife. He's committed no crimes. Neighbors respect him. He seems every bit as intelligent as I am, likely more so. He and I share the same aspirations and dreams. I scribbled out a chart, listing our many mutual attributes.

ATTRIBUTES	DADHI	MAX
Physically able	✓	✓
Willing to work	✓	✓
Trained to do a job	✓	✓
Loves family	✓	✓
Sober and drug free	✓	✓
Good reputation	✓	*You tell me*

We have much in common. Then why the disparity? Why does it take Dadhi a year to earn what I can spend on a sport coat?

Part of the complex answer is this: he was born in the wrong place. He is, as Bono said, "an accident of latitude."[5] A latitude void of unemployment insurance, disability payments, college grants, Social Security, and government supplements. A latitude largely vacant of libraries, vaccinations, clean water, and paved roads. I benefited from each of those. Dadhi has none of them.

In the game of life, many of us who cross home plate do so because we were born on third base. Others aren't even on a team.

You don't have to travel sixteen hours in a plane to find a Dadhi or two. They live in the convalescent home you pass on the way to work, gather at the unemployment office on the corner. They are the poor, the brokenhearted, the captives, and the blind.

Some people are poor because they are lazy. They need to get off their duffs. Others, however, are poor because parasites weaken their bodies, because they spend six hours a day collecting water, because rebel armies ravaged their farms, or because AIDS took their parents.

Couldn't such people use a bit of Jubilee? Of course they could. So ...

First, let the church act on behalf of the poor. The apostles did. "So the Twelve called a meeting of all the believers" (Acts 6:2, NLT). They assembled the entire church. The problem of inequity warranted a churchwide conversation. The leaders wanted every member to know that this church took poverty seriously. The ultimate solution to poverty is found in the compassion of God's people. Scripture endorses not forced communism but Spirit-led volunteerism among God's people.

Second, let the brightest among us direct us. "And so, brothers, select seven men who are well respected and are full of the Spirit and wisdom. We will give them this responsibility" (v. 3, NLT).

The first church meeting led to the first task force. The apostles unleashed their best people on their biggest problem. The challenge demands this. "Poverty," as Rich Stearns, president of World Vision in the United States, told me, "is rocket science." Simple solutions simply don't exist. Most of us don't know what to do about the avalanche of national debt, the withholding of life-saving medicines, the corruption at the seaports, and the abduction of children. Most of us don't know what to do, but someone does!

Some people are pouring every ounce of God-given wisdom into the resolution of these problems. We need specialist organizations, such as World Vision, Compassion International, Living Water, and the International Justice Mission. We need our brightest and best to continue the legacy of the Jerusalem task force of Acts 6.

And one more idea. Get ticked off. Riled up enough to respond. Righteous anger would do a world of good. Poverty is not the lack of charity but the lack of justice. Why do two of us have eight cows while the rest of us have two? Why do a billion people go to bed hungry every night?[6] Why do nearly thirty thousand children die every day, one every three seconds, from hunger and preventable diseases?[7] It's just not fair. Why not do something about it?

Again, no one can do everything, but everyone can do something. Some people can fast and pray about social sin. Others can study and speak out.

What about you? Get out of your comfort zone, for Christ's sake. Why not teach an inner-city Bible study? Use your vacation to build houses in hurricane-ravaged towns? Run for public office? Help a farmer get an ox?

Speaking of which, I received a note from Dadhi the other day. It included a photo of him and a new family member. A new three-hundred-pound, four-legged family member. Both of them were smiling. I'm thinking God was too.

Max Lucado

"Pure and genuine religion in the sight of God the Father means caring for orphans and widows in their distress and refusing to let the world corrupt you." **JAMES 1:27, NLT**

PRAYER

Dear Lord, Jesus promised that we would always have the poor among us. Help me make sure that the reverse is also true, that I am always among the poor—helping, encouraging, and lending a hand wherever I can. Enable me to love the invisible God by serving the very visible poor in my corner of the world. Help me to be creative without being condescending, encouraging without being egotistical, fearless without being foolish. May the poor bless You because of me, and may my efforts somehow reduce the number of the poor. In Jesus' name I pray, amen.

Excerpt from Outlive Your Life *(Nashville: Thomas Nelson, 2010), chapter 10.*

MORE PEOPLE, MORE PROBLEMS

Things were going well in the early church. Thanks to the day of Pentecost and the extraordinary invasion of the Holy Spirit, momentum was on the side of the disciples. Scripture tells us about three thousand people were added to the fellowship of Christians. And these people were devoted.

> **Read the description of those first days in Acts 2:41-47. Which phrase seems most like your own experience in church? Which phrase is least like your experience?**

> **What do you think the emotional climate was like in the midst of the believers during that time?**

What amazing words. What an amazing picture. There must have been an incredible sense of expectation. They had seen the miraculous at Pentecost, and the power of God continued to be demonstrated as more and more people were converted to belief in Christ (see Acts 4:32-36). People must have walked around with a skip in their step and a sparkle in their eyes because they simply didn't know what would happen next. What was God going to show up and do today? No one knew for sure.

Then, in Acts 6, something happened that threatened to kill the movement. Though they had faced external pressure and some measure of persecution even in their brief existence, this time the issue came from within.

Read Acts 6:1. In your own words, what was the problem? Why do you think this particular group was neglected?

What about you? What groups of people are you most likely to overlook?

BOTH/AND

The church was providing regularly for the needs of the Jewish widows, but these Greek-speaking widows were even further off the grid. They weren't receiving any of the attention their situation warranted. And the church recognized the gap in their vision.

Likewise, there are certain groups of people in all our lives who sit in our blind spot. Perhaps we have some long-held prejudices against a certain ethnicity. Or maybe we have some preconceived ideas about why this certain demographic came to be in the situation they're in. But for whatever the reason, there exists in all of us certain areas of blindness to injustice. The church had no choice but to respond. They knew instantly that their faith demanded it. The God of their faith demanded it.

Read Acts 6:2-3. Where do you see the balance between proclamation and social action in this passage? Which would you be more apt to neglect: the widows or the Word?

Can you think of someone who holds this balance well in their life? Describe their lifestyle below.

It's not either/or. It's both/and. The disciples had the wisdom to see the balance. The church needed to be fed both spiritually and physically, and one should not be neglected for the sake of the other. The disciples would continue the work they were doing, but they would make sure that the work of the church included the care for the neglected. It should not be lost on us that the first task force of the church was to deal with the issues of the poor.

The disciples committed themselves to making sure no one—no one—fell through the cracks. It's a cry that James took up in his book a bit later on.

> **Read James 5:1-6. If God is so serious about how the poor are treated, then why are we so quick to overlook them?**

> **Think about your daily schedule. Make a list below of the times you might possibly come in personal contact with a person on the fringes.**

The mandate is clear: There are no exceptions in the mind of God. No one falls through the cracks. The believing community must accept it to be true.

If the church wants to truly follow the example of Jesus, then there's only one way to go: down.

PRAYER

Father, we confess that we do not often care as deeply as You do about people. We confess our contentment to not see the plight of others. Would You open our eyes? Would You open our hearts? We want to think, feel, and act in ways that matter. In Jesus' name I pray, amen.

Day 3
JESUS AT THE BOTTOM

JESUS AND THE POOR

The Jerusalem church had a decision to make, a decision of priorities. They were growing in notoriety and numbers, grace and good will. By the day, the Lord was adding more to their numbers. Then came this question of neglected widows, of the people on the fringe.

Surely the leadership team had more important things to think about. Polity and structure? Perhaps the purchase of a building to house their fellowship? The education of their children and youth? All fine points that needed to be discussed. But they refused to push the issue of the poor and neglected to the back burner because they knew that's not what their Master would have done.

From the beginning of His ministry, Jesus made it clear how He felt about the have-nots. Imagine the scene recorded in Luke 4. The chapter begins in the wilderness, with the Son of God being tempted by Satan. Jesus fasted for 40 days, yet He was strong in faith. Having rejected the temptations of the Devil, He launched into ministry, and it didn't take long for the word to get out. An extraordinary new teacher burst onto the scene. He spoke with power and authority, and it was amazing to see. News and rumors abounded. The crowds began to grow. Jesus was acclaimed by everyone who heard Him.

Then came the news that He would be returning to Nazareth; He was going to speak at the synagogue.

> **What do you think the atmosphere was like in the synagogue on the day Jesus returned?**

> Read Luke 4:16-23. Why do you think Jesus chose this
> passage? What does His choice reveal about His priorities?

Jesus left no doubt as to His priorities: the declaration of freedom, good news, and end of oppression for the prisoners, the blind, the poor, and the outcast. He chose to read a quotation from Isaiah 61, a messianic passage. The people knew this stuff was supposed to happen when the Messiah was in their midst. And here stood Jesus, from right here in Nazareth, saying that at long last, this Scripture has been fulfilled.

"I'M HERE."

They could scarcely believe it. Could it be true? They were in equal parts excited and confused. They had heard the rumors, and Jesus had not disappointed them. But there was still a tinge of doubt in their hearts. This was the little boy, after all, who had grown up down the street. He had played with them, or at least with their children. He had worked in His father's shop. Really? This was the Messiah?

But Jesus, in His surprising way of doing things, couldn't leave well enough alone. He had impressed the crowd. They were all speaking well of Him. But then He went on.

> Read Luke 4:23-30. Why do you think Jesus brought up these
> other stories of the Old Testament?

> What do you notice about the temperament of the people?
> Why do you think it changed so drastically so quickly?

The people's vision was limited. They had a very specific idea about exactly what this Messiah would do and be. He was the people of Israel's Savior. He was coming for them. And yet Jesus talked about an unfortunate (from their perspective) pair of incidents in the lives of the prophets that demonstrated the far-reaching purpose of the Messiah.

There was a time when there was much suffering in Israel. And yet Elijah was sent outside its borders, to a foreign widow from a place called Zarephath in the notoriously wicked land of Sidon. Elisha didn't fare much better—though many people were afflicted with leprosy in Israel, he healed Naaman the Syrian, a foreigner.

And the people were appalled. How could it be so? This is *our* Messiah. Not theirs. They were so angry, in fact, that the mood went from jubilant to violent in a matter of minutes. The same crowd that had been praising Him drove Him to the edge of a cliff with the intent of throwing Him off.

It's dangerous business to offend people's pride.

> **Why would Jesus' statements have offended the pride of those present?**

> **Have you ever been offended by Jesus' commitment to the lowest and the least? Why or why not?**

THOSE PEOPLE, TOO?

It's OK if Jesus wants to help us. That's great. Help us with sickness. Help us with financial troubles. By all means, help us with salvation. But there are certain people we consider to be off limits. Certain ones who don't deserve the attention of the Lord. Our pride prevents us from seeing that Jesus is going to those people, too.

He's going low. He's going to the bottom. He's going to places where we wouldn't be caught dead. That's who He is.

The biggest obstacle to following Jesus is our pride. We consider ourselves too clean, too upright, and too moral to step in the muck and mire of humanity. There are certain places, like Sidon, where we wouldn't dare set foot. What would people say?

We hide behind calling, responsibility, and safety, but in the end it's pride that keeps us high on our supposed societal ladder. But not Jesus. Jesus went low, and His descent was far greater than ours ever will be. From the throne of heaven to the manger. From the adoration of angels to the degradation of men. From the King of the Universe to the cross of a criminal.

The people reacted swiftly and violently in Luke 4, intending to throw Jesus off a hill. But "passing through the midst of them, He went on His way" (Luke 4:28-30).

I wonder if Jesus is still doing the same thing. We turn violent in our pride, unwilling to believe that maybe Jesus is really associating with those people. He doesn't argue with us. He doesn't beg us to come. Rather, He simply passes right through our crowds and goes on His way. He leaves us behind on the cliff because He has little time for the prideful.

They can stay on the hill. He's going lower.

PRAYER

Surely You are the God of the poor in spirit, those who know their great need. Thank You that in reality, we are all poor and in desperate need of You. Rob us of the pride that would seek to separate us from those who are poor in lifestyle. In Jesus' name I pray, amen.

Day 4:
THE KITCHEN TABLE

JUBILEE

As recorded in Luke 4, Jesus stepped to the front of the crowd's attention and opened the scroll. With no quaver in His voice or question in His mind, He declared His priorities. Among His statements was a reference to the year of the Lord's favor. Jesus declared a time of Jubilee was coming.

> **What was the most surprising fact about the year of Jubilee you have learned this week?**

> **Why do you think the people of Israel never practiced the custom?**

> **What does the year of Jubilee indicate about God's character?**

Jubilee is a firm indication about God's desire to keep a close proximity between those who have much and those who have little. Funny that we now work hard at doing the opposite.

> **Why do you think God would be interested in keeping a close proximity between the have's and the have-not's?**

What are some ways we work to keep those two groups apart?
Why do you think we work hard at doing something God
wants to keep from happening?

There is another way in which the principles of Jubilee should be instituted into our lives. It's one that doesn't necessarily involve the wiping away of debt or the unshackling of leg irons. We can practice Jubilee with nothing more than a kitchen table.

HOSPITALITY

God wants His children to be people of hospitality.

Let's define the word. What does "hospitality" mean to you?

Describe one instance below when someone showed you
hospitality. What made that particular instance stand out
in your mind?

Long before the church had pulpits and baptisteries, she had kitchens and dinner tables. "The believers met together in the Temple every day. They ate together in their homes, happy to share their food with joyful hearts" (Acts 2:46, NCV). "Every day in the Temple and in people's homes they continued teaching the people and telling the Good News—that Jesus is the Christ" (Acts 5:42, NCV).

Even a casual reading of the New Testament unveils the house as the primary tool of the church. "To Philemon our beloved friend and fellow laborer ... and to the church in your house" (Philem. 1-2). "Greet Priscilla and Aquila ... the church that is in their house" (Rom. 16:3,5). "Greet the brethren who are in Laodicea, and Nymphas and the church that is in his house" (Col. 4:15).

Why would the early church have been so committed to using their homes? What sorts of things does that willingness demonstrate?

Part of it was necessity. There was simply nowhere else to meet. There were no building funds. No classrooms. No childcare facilities. No video screens. The only option for the fledgling church was homes. But meeting in that setting was actually the perfect incubator for growth in Christ to take place.

Consider what the gospel is fundamentally about: We were sick. Dying. Imprisoned by sin. Outside of the family of God. But God opened up His home and His heart to us. He took us in out of the cold, sat us down at His table, and gave us something to eat. He welcomed us in. The church's commitment to open their homes demonstrated the same principle.

GETTING CLOSER

See, when you're trying to stand up for the have-nots, you can easily default into treating them as a "service project." God will have none of that. Not for His hospitable children.

Hospitality is the realm in which "they" stop being "they" and all of us start being "we." When we provide food stamps, we stave off hunger. But when we invite the hungry to our table, we address the deeper issues of value and self-worth. Who would have thought? God's secret weapons in the war on poverty include your kitchen table and mine.

That's what hospitality is. It's not as much inviting people into your home (although it would be difficult to accomplish it without doing so) as it is inviting people into your life.

What's the difference between inviting people into your home and inviting people into your life?

What is the scariest part about this type of hospitality to you?

Is your life currently set up for hospitality? What might need to change in order for you to practice hospitality?

What will it take for us to actually offer ourselves in the spirit of true hospitality? It's a risk no doubt. At the very least, it's inconvenient. It's a burden. At least at first. It will take some rearranging of schedules. A few extra plates at the table. The lowering of our defenses. A listening ear. But we can do it because it has been done for us. God has welcomed us into His house when we had nothing to bring with us. He brought us in and sat us at His table. We can do the same for others.

Open your table. Open your life.

PRAYER

Thank You, Father, for modeling true hospitality for us. Thank You for swinging open the doors of Your heavenly home to welcome the poor, dirty, and sinful. How can we do any less? Make our homes places where people are welcomed, fed, and nurtured with the love of Christ. In Jesus' name I pray, amen.

Do Good. Quietly.

Right Thing, Wrong Reason

Stand up for the have-nots. That was the practice of Jesus, and that was the practice of the early church. From Acts 6 on, the church demonstrated its fundamental belief that to be a follower of Jesus meant following Him to the bottom, caring for the lowest and the least one might find there. And yet, the human heart is a strange thing. It is disconcerting to acknowledge that we may, at points, do the right thing for all the wrong reasons. We can involve ourselves in the ministries of Jesus, but we may do so for selfish gain. The Lord knew this, and so He gave some very practical advice in the Sermon on the Mount.

> **Read Matthew 6:1-4. Draw a picture below of the kind of person Jesus is describing.**

It's wonderful to be committed to giving to the poor. Visiting the prisoners. Clothing the needy. But we must proceed with caution: the heart is deceitful above all things. Let's make sure we're going forward for the right reasons.

Owners or Stewards?

That's some advice a couple named Ananias and Sapphira really needed to hear. Leading up to their story is a beautiful description of the activity of the early church.

Read Acts 4:32-37. Why do you think these early believers were able to take such a radical stance in regard to their property?

Before we attribute an early form of communism to the first believers, we should look a little deeper into what fueled them. They evidently had become convinced of a simple truth that often eludes us in the midst of our search for the newest and best thing to add to our list of many possessions: God is the owner of all.

Everything is His. All the money. All the technology. He holds the universal patent. If it's all His, then we aren't really owners; we are stewards. We have been entrusted with what we have. Whether intelligence or talents or material possessions, everything has been given to us by God to put to use.

Make a list below of three things that you own and three things that you steward. How is your attitude different toward each list?

Own	Steward
1.	1.
2.	2.
3.	3.

When we recognize God as the true owner, we are freed to give liberally. We are loosed from the consumer bonds of selfishness in order to be productive members of the kingdom of God.

What are three things in your life that you would have trouble acknowledging that God owns? Why those three things?

1.

2.

3.

Ananias and Sapphira

The story of Ananias and Sapphira becomes all the more stark when set against this backdrop. Evidently, they got caught up in the giving spirit, and then logic took hold. They realized that they weren't quite as committed to the ownership of God as they thought.

Read the story of Ananias and Sapphira in Acts 5:1-11. Does God's reaction seem extreme to you? Why or why not?

Ananias and Sapphira deserved punishment, for sure. They deserved a stiff sentence. But the death sentence? Does the punishment fit the crime? What they did was bad, but was it that bad? Let's think about it. Exactly what did they do? They used the church for self-promotion. They leveraged God's family for personal gain. They attempted to turn a congregation into a personal stage across which they could strut. God has a strong word for such behavior: hypocrisy.

Read Matthew 23:5-25. Why do you think God reacts so strongly to hypocrisy?

Jesus never spoke to anyone else with such intensity. He ate and drank with sinners of every kind, but hypocrisy boiled the blood of the Son of God. The Greek word for hypocrite originally meant "actor." First-century actors wore masks. A hypocrite, then, is one who puts on a mask, a false face.

What are a few practical ways you might guard against hypocrisy in doing good?

Jesus did not say, "Do not do good works." Nor did He instruct, "Do not let your works be seen." We must do good works, and some works, such as benevolence or teaching, must be seen in order to have an impact. So let's be clear. To do good is good. To do good to be seen is not. Here's why.

Hypocrisy turns people away from God. When God-hungry souls walk into a congregation of wannabe superstars, what happens? When God seekers hear the preacher play to the crowd and exclude God … When other attendees dress to be seen and draw attention to their gifts and offerings … When people enter a church to see God yet can't see God because of the church, don't think for a second that God doesn't react.

Hypocrisy turns people against God. So God has a no-tolerance policy. Let the cold, lifeless bodies of the embezzling couple issue their intended warning. Let's take hypocrisy as seriously as God does.

Let's do good. Quietly.

PRAYER

How deceptive are our human hearts? We need You, Father, to show us the motivation behind the good we seek to do. Move us toward purity in motive as well as action. In Jesus' name I pray, amen.

OUTLIVING YOUR LIFE THIS WEEK

Scripture Memory: "Pure and genuine religion in the sight of God the Father means caring for orphans and widows in their distress and refusing to let the world corrupt you" (Jas. 1:27, NLT).

Action Plan: This week find out more about what your church is already doing in the midst of the poor and neglected. Volunteer to get involved personally. If you see a gap in your church's care, volunteer to begin exploring how that gap might be filled.

WEEK 5

BLAST
A FEW
WALLS

GROUP REVIEW OF WEEK 4

What one truth sticks out from the study this week? What practical changes do you think God is calling you to make based on this week of study?

Look back at the Action Plan for week 4 on page 116. What was the most meaningful and impacting part of that activity for you? Why?

Do you think our churches generally reflect God's commitment to the least of these? Why or why not?

What do you think is the main thing standing in the way of us having a great commitment in our churches to helping those in need?

Describe your last encounter with the poor, hungry, or homeless. Are forming relationships with people in such situations comfortable or uncomfortable for you? Why?

Is your life geared toward encountering them or avoiding them? What might have to change in order for you to come in more regular contact with them?

VIEW DVD MESSAGE
"BLAST A FEW WALLS"

When we help _____ , we help _____ .

> "Philip went down to the city of Samaria and preached Christ to them. And the multitudes with one accord heeded the things spoken by Philip, hearing and seeing the miracles which he did. For unclean spirits, crying with a loud voice, came out of many who were possessed; and many who were paralyzed and lame were healed" (Acts 8:5-7).

> "... when they had come down, prayed for them that they might receive the Holy Spirit. For as yet He had fallen upon none of them. They had only been baptized in the name of the Lord Jesus. Then they laid hands on them, and they received the Holy Spirit" (Acts 8:15-17).

God is celebrating the falling of a wall.

ETHIOPIAN	PHILIP
_____ - _____	Light-skinned
Foreign	Local
Powerful	_____
Eunuch	Father of four

> "Philip said, 'If you believe with all your heart, you may.' And he answered and said, 'I believe that Jesus Christ is the Son of God'" (Acts 8:37).

Acts 8 teaches us how God feels about the person on the other side of the _____ .

"Christ brought us together through his death on the cross. The Cross got us to embrace, and that was the end of the hostility" (Eph. 2:16, Message).

The United States will soon be the most _____ _____ nation in all of history.

When we cross the field and cheer for the other side, _____ wins.

This session is available for download at *www.lifeway.com/downloads.*

GROUP RESPONSE

What sort of spiritual benefit do you get when you help the poor, the people with whom Jesus identifies so closely?

What sorts of obstacles might have kept the early church from extending to Samaria? Why do you think Jesus specifically mentioned this area in Acts 1:8?

Why do you think God is committed to breaking down walls?

Do you think we feel the same way about cultural walls or that we like them? Why?

How do you think Christians should respond to the racial diversity of the United States? How do we currently respond?

Day 1
BLAST A FEW WALLS

Fans rooted for the competition. Cheerleaders switched loyalties. The coach helped the opposition score points. Parents yelled for the competition. What was this?

This was the brainchild of a big-hearted football coach in Grapevine, Texas. Kris Hogan skippers the successful program of Faith Christian High School. He has seventy players, eleven coaches, quality equipment, and parents who care, make banners, attend pep rallies, and wouldn't miss a game for their own funeral.

They took their 7–2 record into a contest with Gainesville State School. Gainesville's players, by contrast, wear seven-year-old shoulder pads and last decade's helmets and show up at each game wearing handcuffs. Their parents don't watch them play, but twelve uniformed officers do. That's because Gainesville is a maximum-security correctional facility. The school doesn't have a stadium, cheerleading squad, or half a hope of winning. Gainesville was 0–8 going into the Grapevine game. They'd scored two touchdowns all year.

The whole situation didn't seem fair. So Coach Hogan devised a plan. He asked the fans to step across the field and, for one night only, to cheer for the other side. More than two hundred volunteered. They formed a forty-yard spirit line. They painted "Go Tornadoes!" on a banner that the Gainesville squad could burst through. They sat on the Gainesville side of the stadium. They even learned the names of Gainesville players so they could yell for individuals.

The prisoners had heard people scream their names but never like this. Gerald, a lineman who will serve three years, said, "People are a little afraid of us when we come to the games. You can see it in their eyes. They're lookin' at us like we're criminals. But these people, they were yellin' for us. By our names!"

After the game the teams gathered in the middle of the field to say a prayer. One of the incarcerated players asked to lead it. Coach Hogan agreed, not knowing what to expect. "Lord," the boy said, "I don't know how this happened, so

I don't know how to say thank you, but I never would've known there was so many people in the world that cared about us." Grapevine fans weren't finished. After the game they waited beside the Gainesville bus to give each player a good-bye gift—burger, fries, candy, soda, a Bible, an encouraging letter, and a round of applause. As their prison bus left the parking lot, the players pressed stunned faces against the windows and wondered what had just hit them.[1]

Here's what hit them: a squad of bigotry-demolition experts. Their assignment? Blast bias into dust. Their weapons? A fusillade of "You still matter" and "Someone still cares." Their mission? Break down barricades that separate God's children from each other.

Do any walls bisect your world? There you stand on one side. And on the other? The person you've learned to disregard, perhaps even disdain. The teen with the tats. The boss with the bucks. The immigrant with the hard-to-understand accent. The person on the opposite side of your political fence. The beggar who sits outside your church every week. Or the Samaritans outside Jerusalem.

Talk about a wall, ancient and tall. "Jews," as John wrote in his Gospel, "refuse to have anything to do with Samaritans" (John 4:9, NLT). The two cultures had hated each other for a thousand years. The feud involved claims of defection, intermarriage, and disloyalty to the temple. Samaritans were blacklisted. Their beds, utensils—even their spittle—were considered unclean.[2] No orthodox Jew would travel into the region. Most Jews would gladly double the length of their trip rather than go through Samaria.

Jesus, however, played by a different set of rules. He spent the better part of a day on the turf of a Samaritan woman, drinking water from her ladle, discussing her questions (John 4:1-26). He stepped across the cultural taboo as if it were a sleeping dog in the doorway. Jesus loves to break down walls. That's why he sent Philip to Samaria.

> "Then Philip went down to the city of Samaria and preached
> Christ to them. And the multitudes with one accord heeded the
> things spoken by Philip, hearing and seeing the miracles which

he did. For unclean spirits, crying with a loud voice, came out of many who were possessed; and many who were paralyzed and lame were healed … When they believed Philip as he preached the things concerning the kingdom of God and the name of Jesus Christ, both men and women were baptized" (Acts 8:5-7,12).

The city broke out into a revival. Peter and John heard about the response and traveled from Jerusalem to Samaria to confirm it. "When they had come down, [they] prayed for them that they might receive the Holy Spirit. For as yet He had fallen upon none of them. They had only been baptized in the name of the Lord Jesus. Then they laid hands on them, and they received the Holy Spirit" (vv. 15-17).

This is a curious turn of events. Why hadn't the Samaritans received the Holy Spirit? On the day of Pentecost, Peter promised the gift of the Spirit to those who repented and were baptized. How then can we explain the baptism of the Samaritans, which, according to Luke, was not accompanied by the Spirit? Why delay the gift?

Simple. To celebrate the falling of a wall. The gospel, for the first time, was breaching an ancient bias. God marked the moment with a ticker-tape parade of sorts. He rolled out the welcome mat and sent His apostles to verify the revival and place hands on the Samaritans. Let any doubt be gone: God accepts all people. But He wasn't finished. He sent Philip on a second cross-cultural mission.

"Now an angel of the Lord spoke to Philip, saying, 'Arise and go toward the south along the road which goes down from Jerusalem to Gaza.' This is desert. So he arose and went. And behold, a man of Ethiopia, a eunuch of great authority under Candace the queen of the Ethiopians, who had charge of all her treasury, and had come to Jerusalem to worship, was returning. And sitting in his chariot, he was reading Isaiah the prophet. Then the Spirit said to Philip, 'Go near and overtake this chariot' " (vv. 26-29).

Walls separated Philip from the eunuch. The Ethiopian was dark skinned; Philip was light. The official hailed from distant Africa; Philip grew up nearby.

The traveler was rich enough to travel. And who was Philip but a simple refugee, banished from Jerusalem? And don't overlook the delicate matter of differing testosterone levels. Philip, we later learn, was the father of four girls (Acts 21:9). The official was a eunuch. No wife or kids or plans for either. The lives of the two men could not have been more different.

But Philip didn't hesitate. He "preached Jesus to him. Now as they went down the road, they came to some water. And the eunuch said, 'See, here is water. What hinders me from being baptized?' " (Acts 8:35-36). No small question. A black, influential, effeminate official from Africa turns to the white, simple, virile Christian from Jerusalem and asks, "Is there any reason I can't have what you have?"

What if Philip had said, "Now that you mention it, yes. Sorry. We don't take your type"? But Philip, charter member of the bigotry-demolition team, blasted through the wall:, " 'If you believe with all your heart, you may.' And he answered and said, 'I believe that Jesus Christ is the Son of God' " (v. 37). Next thing you know, the eunuch is stepping out of the baptism waters, whistling "Jesus Loves Me," Philip is on to his next assignment, and the church has her first non-Jewish convert.

And we are a bit dizzy. What do we do with a chapter like this? Samaria. Peter and John arriving. Holy Spirit falling. Gaza. Ethiopian official. Philip. What do these events teach us? They teach us how God feels about the person on the other side of the wall.

> "He tore down the wall we used to keep each other at a distance. ... Instead of continuing with two groups of people separated by centuries of animosity and suspicion, he created a new kind of human being, a fresh start for everybody. ... Christ brought us together through his death on the Cross. The Cross got us to embrace, and that was the end of the hostility" (Eph. 2:14-16, Message).

The cross of Christ creates a new people, a people unhindered by skin color or family feud. A new citizenry based, not on common ancestry or geography, but on a common Savior.

My friend Buckner Fanning experienced this firsthand. He was a marine in World War II, stationed in Nagasaki three weeks after the dropping of the atomic bomb. Can you imagine a young American soldier amid the rubble and wreckage of the demolished city? Radiation-burned victims wandering the streets. Atomic fallout showering on the city. Bodies burned to a casket black. Survivors shuffling through the streets, searching for family, food, and hope. The conquering soldier feeling not victory but grief for the suffering around him.

Instead of anger and revenge, Buckner found an oasis of grace. While patrolling the narrow streets, he came upon a sign that bore an English phrase: Methodist Church. He noted the location and resolved to return the next Sunday morning. When he did, he entered a partially collapsed structure. Windows, shattered. Walls, buckled. The young marine stepped through the rubble, unsure how he would be received. Fifteen or so Japanese were setting up chairs and removing debris. When the uniformed American entered their midst, they stopped and turned.

He knew only one word in Japanese. He heard it. Brother. "They welcomed me as a friend," Buckner relates, the power of the moment still resonating more than sixty years after the events. They offered him a seat. He opened his Bible and, not understanding the sermon, sat and observed. During communion the worshipers brought him the elements. In that quiet moment the enmity of their nations and the hurt of the war was set aside as one Christian served another the body and blood of Christ. Another wall came a-tumblin' down.

What walls are in your world? Brian Overcast is knocking down walls in Morelia, Mexico. As director of the NOÉ Center (New Opportunities in Education), Brian and his team address the illegal immigration problem from a unique angle. Staff members told me recently, "Mexicans don't want to cross the border. If they could stay home, they would. But they can't because they can't get jobs. So we teach them English. With English skills they can get accepted into one of Mexico's low-cost universities and find a career at home. Others see illegal immigrants; we see opportunities." Another wall down.

We can't outlive our lives if we can't get beyond our biases. Who are your Samaritans? Ethiopian eunuchs? Whom have you been taught to distrust and avoid? It's time to remove a few bricks. Welcome the day God takes you to your

Samaria—not so distant in miles but different in styles, tastes, tongues, and traditions. And if you meet an Ethiopian eunuch, so different yet so sincere, don't refuse that person. Don't let class, race, gender, politics, geography, or culture hinder God's work. For the end of the matter is this: when we cross the field and cheer for the other side, everyone wins.

Max Lucado

"Therefore, accept each other just as Christ has accepted you so that God will be given glory." ROMANS 15:7, NLT

PRAYER

Lord, in how many ways does my foolish heart make false distinctions among Your people? Reveal them to me. How often do I judge someone as unworthy of You by the way I treat him or her? Rebuke me in Your love. Where can I blast a wall or remove a barrier that keeps Your children apart from one another? Give me some dynamite and the skill and courage to use it for Your glory. What can I do in my sphere of influence to bring the love of Christ to someone who may feel ostracized or estranged from You? Lend me divine insight, and bless me with the resolve to be Your hands and feet. May I be a bridge and not a wall. In Jesus' name I pray, amen.

Excerpt from Outlive Your Life *(Nashville: Thomas Nelson, 2010), chapter 12.*

LET THE WALLS COME DOWN

A WAITING DEMOLITION SQUAD

Jesus intended the early church to be a squad of bigotry-demolition experts. But the breaking down of societal walls is a messy business. It involves risk and hardship, discomfort and challenge.

Jesus had given the early church the cross-cultural directive of Acts 1:8, but He had bolstered their sagging confidence in their ability to complete their worldwide mission by promising power from on high.

Wait. Not yet. Go, but not until you are equipped. And when you are equipped with the Spirit, then begin to spread. Start in Jerusalem, but don't stop there. Branch out to places you never would have thought about going before.

Holy Spirit? Check. Pentecost came in a flash, and it was world-changing. Early church up and running? Check. Meetings were happening regularly, and the leadership recognized that they needed to reach out to the have-nots. The gospel was being preached and lived out in their midst. But go? No check. Stalled. In fact, when we come to Acts 8, six chapters after the coming of the Holy Spirit, relatively little had been done in terms of moving out. The church was still centered in Jerusalem.

Why do you think they had not moved out yet?

What are some of the ways we justify our own refusal to move out into relationships and interactions with people who are different than we are?

Whatever the reason, they had not yet gone. They had limited themselves to Jerusalem, and because they had, they were not yet the wall-busters God planned for them to be. In fact, it took a set of tragic circumstances for the disciples to embrace their international calling.

> Read Acts 7:54–8:8. In your own words, what happened to Stephen? Where do you see the redemptive hand of God at work in the midst of this tragedy?

> Can you think of a time when you have experienced some sort of tragic circumstance only to realize that God was using it for the multiplication of the gospel?

Stephen was dead. One of the best and brightest new Christians had his life snuffed out. And that was only the beginning. A wave of persecution swept through the church. But instead of squelching this new religion, we see God using this tragedy for good. The persecution was the spark of international mission, and at last the church was on the move. Specifically, the church was on the move to Samaria.

SAMARIA

Here was a region Jesus specifically mentioned in His cross-cultural marching orders of Acts 1:8. But moving into that area would require the break down of some long existing walls for the early church.

> Based on your reading from day 1, what were the major cultural walls that existed between Jews and Samaritans?

What similar walls are there in your world? Who is your
Samaritan?

But fueled by calling and prompted by necessity, Philip found himself in the
confines of this long-hated region. But then the strangest thing happened.

Read Acts 8:5-12. Why do you think Philip was granted the
ability to do so many things?

How might that ability have served the purpose of breaking
down walls?

The Samaritan experience serves as an example of God's desire for walls to fall
down. His plan is to deconstruct those carefully built bricks of bias in order to
create something new and different out of the rubble.

Read Ephesians 2:14-16. Do you typically think about the
cross bringing together God and humanity or humanity to
each other? Why?

In what sense does the cross bring people together?

THE ACTUAL WALL

There was a literal dividing wall that might have been in Paul's mind as he wrote
Ephesians 2. The temple was the center of the religious life of the worshiper
of Yahweh. That's where the sacrifices were made, and that was where God

was said to dwell. Both Jews and God-fearing Gentiles would come to the complex, all were armed with doves or pigeons or lambs—whatever they could afford. They all knew their sin had to be atoned for. But there was a key difference between the two groups. The structure of the temple was a series of concentric areas. The initial ring, the farthest to the outside of the complex, was called the court of the Gentiles. Anyone could go there. But the Gentiles could go no farther. They were restricted to that area. Only ethnic Jews could proceed farther, symbolically moving more into the presence of God. There was a literal wall that separated the ethnic groups.

> **Put yourself in the place of a God-fearing Gentile. What would go through your mind as you looked at the wall?**

> **What about if you were a devout Jew? How do you think you would look at the wall as you passed beyond it?**

I wonder if the Gentiles looked at the wall longingly, and yet with a little bit of bitter contempt. They would like to go deeper, but they were restricted to the outside. Not because of their conduct but because of their ethnicity. Nothing else. There was a barrier that kept them out as outsiders. Strangers. Aliens.

For the Jews, meanwhile, the wall served as a confidence-booster. It was a reminder of their special status. They might not be living rightly, but at least they weren't staying on the outside. At least they had a ticket in the door. But Jesus changed all that.

A New Race

Paul said that God was building a new race. One new man out of the many races of the earth. It's the race of Christianity. And that makes sense when you think about it.

Jesus described entrance into the kingdom of God as such a drastic change that it is being born again (see John 3:1-8). When we were born the first time, we were born into a specific family. A specific nationality. A specific race. Why should the second time be any different? Peter learned through his encounter with a God-fearing Gentile named Cornelius (see Acts 10) that God shows no favoritism when it comes to entering His family.

> **Read 1 Peter 2:9-10. Make a list below of the terms Peter used to describe believers.**

The believing community supersedes race and creed and origin. People may still be black or white or brown, but they are now "Christians." That is their defining characteristic, even more defining than their place of birth.

The Samaritan city broke out into a revival. Peter and John heard about the response and traveled from Jerusalem to Samaria to confirm it. And suddenly all doubt is gone: God accepts all people. Shouldn't we do the same?

PRAYER

Father, You are the great Unifier. You have brought together one new race out of all the peoples of the earth. Help us begin to see ourselves not as black, white, brown, or anything else before we see ourselves as Christians. In Jesus' name I pray, amen.

PREACHING JESUS

Philip went where few Jews sat foot, and even fewer did so on purpose. He scaled the wall built on centuries of cultural and societal bias and then ripped it down, brick by brick. Thanks to Philip and the validation from Peter and John, the early church was on the move.

And it was moving out.

But just when you think Philip had put in a full day's work with his Samaritan wall-demolishing, the Holy Spirit sent him on a second cross-cultural mission.

> Read Acts 8:26-36. Based on your previous reading, what
> were some of the walls separating Philip from the Ethiopian?
> Which do you think would be the most difficult to overcome?

> Who would be equivalent of the Ethiopian eunuch to you?

> Do you think we, as Christians today, "preach Jesus"? What else
> might we have the tendency to preach in addition to Jesus?

It's a very short but descriptive phrase isn't it? Notice that Philip didn't preach church membership. Or behavior change. Or political ideation. He preached Jesus to the Ethiopian eunuch. There might be chances later to preach all those things and some of them might even be appropriate. But right then, he preached Jesus. We would do well to preach a little more Jesus and a little less of our own opinions.

In response, the spiritually sensitive official had a simple question: "Is there any reason I can't have what you have?"

> **How do you think you would have responded if you were in Philip's shoes? What does your answer above reveal about some walls still existing in your life?**

AMBASSADORS
"If you believe with all your heart, you may."

So much jam-packed into that simple response. So much freedom. So much grace. So much compassion. This is the proper response for all those who follow in the footsteps of Jesus, for it is precisely this kind of ministry with which He had entrusted us.

> **Read 2 Corinthians 5:16-20. What do you think it means to look on others in a purely human way?**

> **What, then, is the opposite of that? What does it mean to not know anyone in a purely human way?**

There are certain things that jump immediately to our senses when we meet someone. We notice hair color. Clothing style. Smell. Cleanliness. These are basic observations, but when we make them, we are already creating an internal evaluation of the person standing in front of us. But Paul encouraged us to look past those base appearances and see people differently because of Jesus. We are to have a new perspective on others (not viewing them in a purely human way), on God (we no longer know Him as we did), on life (old things have passed away and new things have come), and even ourselves (we are a new creation). Our entire perspective changes because we have been entirely changed by Jesus.

We are new people with new eyes. A new nose. New taste buds. We must cease making these snap judgments of other human beings and instead begin to see everyone that comes in our path as an image-bearer of God.

> **How would your conversations with others change if you began to see them with a new perspective?**

> **What are three things that stand in the way of you having a new perspective?**
> 1.
>
> 2.
>
> 3.

As we encounter these people, we must allow our new identity as the children of God to influence our perspective on others, the world, and even ourselves. The new person doesn't regard others the way the old person did. We see others as people of value because they were created in the same way we were—in the image of God. That means we treat them with the respect and dignity they deserve.

A MESSAGE OF RECONCILIATION

In a great act of rebellion, people crucified the One who had come to seek and to save. And yet in God's wisdom, that one act resulted in the very thing He was after all along—reconciliation. That was the mission God gave to Jesus:

get My people back. And that's the message we carry with us as ambassadors: be reconciled to God.

> **What is the job description of an ambassador? Which part of that job description would be the most challenging for you? Why?**

An ambassador, by its very definition, is one who is sent as a representative of another political system, king, president, or ruler. As a representative, an ambassador must offer an accurate picture of the ruler, acting always in accordance with the ruler's wishes. That person's whole purpose is to extend the wishes and will of the person, country, or institution they represent in a foreign land.

It would be unthinkable for an ambassador to act in violation of their sending nation's policies and wishes. Yet that's exactly what we do when we hold onto prejudices and internal walls. We violate the wishes of the Sender.

He loves people, and so must we.

PRAYER

You are the God who reconciles, and You have entrusted to us, Your children, that ministry. Thank You for the incredible privilege to speak Your word of grace and peace to the earth. May we not only speak but visibly demonstrate Your great commitment to reconciliation. In Jesus' name I pray, amen.

Help Them. Help Him.

Beyond Distrust

The events of Acts can leave us a little dizzy. The church was waiting ... waiting ... waiting ... Then suddenly there's Philip. A Samaritan revival. An Ethiopian convert. God wrote a story to let us know how He feels about the person on the other side of the wall.

Which is a little awkward for us, because there are certain segments of our own society we have been taught to distrust. For the Jerusalem church, it was the Samaritans. And the Gentiles. For us? It's the rednecks. The kids from the slums. The trailer park residents. The cart-pusher on the corner. The list could go on. But the call of Jesus is clear: Don't be ruled by your preconditioning. Go beyond your distrust. Reach out. You might be surprised who you'll find if you do.

> **What is one segment of the population you've been taught to distrust? What do you think it would be like to have lunch with one of "those" people?**

This was the subject of Jesus' final sermon, recorded in Matthew 25.

Sheep and Goats

Matthew 25 was taught during the final week of Jesus' life. In the same way that a family might gather around the deathbed of a grandfather, the disciples' leaned close to hear these words of their teacher. They asked Him to help them understand what would happen at the end of the age, and Jesus responded with a series of stories to help them grasp and be ready for judgment day. All these parables demonstrate the priorities of the kingdom of God.

They are stories illustrating that kingdom people must live with the goals and priorities of the kingdom in mind. The grand finale of that series of teachings is the story of the sheep and the goats.

> **Read Matthew 25:31-46. What are three questions that come to your mind after reading this passage?**
>
> 1.
>
> 2.
>
> 3.

In this story, Jesus showed His support, care, and identification with those who are unsupported, neglected, and despised. The hungry. The thirsty. The lonely. The naked. The sick. The prisoners. But how can one envision this moment without the sudden appearance of this urgent question: What determines His choice? How does Jesus separate the people?

> **Does this passage teach that we can earn salvation by treating those in need generously? If not, what does it teach?**

Those on the right, the sheep, will be those who acted on behalf of the lowest and the least. The sign of the saved is their concern for those in need. Compassion does not save them—or us. Salvation is the work of Christ when we believe, apart from our actions. But compassion is the consequence of that salvation.

And amazingly enough, Jesus' words indicate that at this moment, the climactic moment of all history, He will stand beside those who are the lowest and the least.

Which of the people described in Matthew 25 do you identify with the most? What about the least? Why?

He's There

The context is different now, but the hungry, lonely, naked, and sick are still very much among us. The string of unnamed aborted babies. The veterans sleeping under bridges. The aging parents sent to live out their days in nursing homes. The imprisoned minorities. The mentally ill in padded rooms. These are the uncomfortable realities of our world, and they are the ones we pass by, pretending not to notice. Or that we shake our head in sadness but do nothing about. Or that we ship away somewhere out of sight and out of mind.

Unfortunately for us, Jesus goes well beyond just saying that He loves them. He actually claimed, in this passage, to be among them. As one of them.

Do you see Jesus in these kinds of outcasts? Why or why not?

It's truly amazing but very clear: Jesus is so utterly and completely identified with these issues that when we engage with one of those people, we engage Him. Jesus Christ Himself is in the midst of those in great need.

It's the difference between doing those things for Jesus and doing those things to Jesus. He's there in the malnourished and sunken cheeks. He's there in the small underfed body. He's there under the overpass. He's there. If we want to really know Jesus, we had better be there too.

What are the top three things that might have to change in your life if you wanted to regularly associate with the poor?

1.

2.

3.

OMISSION

It's a fact that the goats missed. Take careful notice of this—Jesus didn't berate the goats for what they did wrong. Their great sin wasn't what they did; it was what they failed to do.

> **Do you think we focus more in the church on sins of commission or sins of omission?**

> **Is it easier to focus on one more than the other? Why?**

Jesus is concerned that we refrain from certain things, but oftentimes we focus so much on what we're not supposed to do that we forget about what we are to be engaged in. We are people who are very good at saying no, but the story of the sheep and goats asks us, "What exactly are we saying yes to?"

The Jerusalem church could have been content to avoid sins of commission. But they knew that if they were following Jesus, they had to face the issues of omission as well. Jesus, after all, was going low. To the bottom of society.

They had to go there too.

PRAYER

Father, we want to be the sheep who care and act on behalf of the least of these. We believe that we will find You there, on the bottom rung of the social ladder. Help us not to do these things only because it is our duty but because it is our joy. In Jesus' name I pray, amen.

NOT THAT SAUL

The Samaritans? It's a big wall, but OK. An Ethiopian eunuch? Wow. Very tough to break down that divider, but we'll give it a shot. But Acts 9 takes wall-busting to another level. For it's in Acts 9 that we see yet another wall coming down. This wall is not about ethnicity; nor is it about social position. This is a wall of violence. A wall of past atrocities. A wall of fear.

And the wall was represented by a man named Saul.

> **Read Acts 7:54–8:3. What kind of reputation would Saul have had based on this passage?**

> **Why do you think he was so angry at the church?**

Saul knew a thing or two about being Jewish. He was well versed in the Torah, the Pentateuch, the Prophets, and other sacred books. In fact, he was such a prodigy that he left his home city of Tarsus to study with the great Rabbi, Gamaliel, in Jerusalem.

In his studies, he became more and more zealous for the things of his faith. It was precisely this zealousness that fueled his rage against the early church. In fact, he saw his murderous mission as God-ordained and divinely-supported.

It was about protecting the reputation of his God, a reputation that was being sullied by this new religion. They preached that the Messiah had come and died. On a cross of all things! The thought was unthinkable to Saul. And so he "persecuted the church of God beyond measure and tried to destroy it" (Gal. 1:13). But God had something else in store for Saul.

Read Acts 9:1-9. Is there anything strange about Jesus' words? Who did Jesus say he was persecuting?

Why would Jesus say that?

Focus in on verse 8. What is significant about Saul being struck blind? Why is that a fitting symbol?

Somewhere on this journey Saul was knocked to the ground by a heavenly light. He met Jesus, and he was blinded.

Or was he?

Seeing For the First Time

The blindness was fitting, for his physical abilities were suddenly brought in line with his spiritual sense. Saul had been blind. Like one who missed the forest for the trees, he had immersed himself in the things of God. But in so doing, he had missed the point of all the law. All the prophets. All the sacrifices. All the traditions. He had missed Jesus. But now—having come face-to-face with Jesus, he was blind, and yet he could see for the first time.

What do you think Paul thought about during his three days of blindness?

What do you think his emotional life was like during that time? Why?

His companions rushed to help him. They loaded him on his animal, led him to the inn, and walked him up the stone stairs. By the time Ananias arrived, he'd been here for three days.

Read what happened in Acts 9:10-19. What do you think was going through Ananias's mind as he went to the house?

What is meaningful to you about the way Ananias addressed Saul?

If you were Ananias, what might you have said to him? What could Ananias's attitude have been in the inn that day?

Ananias draws near to Saul and sits. The two stay silent a long time. Ananias takes Saul's hand and feels it tremble. He observes the quivering lips. He sees the sword resting in the corner. Ananias blinks back a tear and realizes that Christ has already broken through the wall. All that remains is for Ananias to clear a few bricks. He began, "Brother Saul ..."

Brother. Not enemy. Not outsider. Not hater. *Brother.* I wonder if Ananias's own lips were quivering as he said the words. In so doing, he was acknowledging the work of God in that place. Saul was blind spiritually, but now he could see. It was left for Ananias to bring the physical in line with the spiritual.

GOD'S LONG ARM

The conversion of Saul stands as a lasting testimony to us that there is no such thing as a lost cause. No one is beyond the long reach of Jesus. That's something we desperately need to be reminded of because we all know a Saul or two.

Who is your "Saul"?

How often do you engage that person in conversation?
How often do you pray for them?

What do your efforts reveal about your confidence in God's reach?

Paul would become the greatest missionary and theologian in the history of the church. In the wake of this turn of events, there is one question I think is worth asking: Where would we be if not for Ananias?

Ananias, who largely disappeared from history. Ananias, who went on to live a quiet life for the Lord. Ananias, who never, so far as we know, wrote a theological letter or traveled widely in missionary efforts.

But Ananias, who was willing to reach out. To take a chance. To call someone "brother" who he only hours before had been taught to fear.

For every Paul there is an Ananias. Someone behind the scenes who first extended a hand. Who engaged in a conversation. Who was willing to trust in the work of the Lord. Who was willing to break down what remained of walls. Who wouldn't give up on a lost cause.

You may not be Paul. He's one in a million. But the chance is there, today, for us all to be Ananias.

PRAYER

You are the God who performs miracles. You did so with each of us, and You continue to do so every moment. May we never see anyone as a lost cause. Bolster our confidence in the power of the gospel, and may we share openly and freely about You, for with You nothing is impossible. In Jesus' name I pray, amen.

OUTLIVING YOUR LIFE THIS WEEK

Scripture Memory: "Accept each other just as Christ has accepted you so that God will be given glory" (Rom. 15:7, NLT).

Action Plan: Grow in your cross-cultural awareness. Learn about the group that lives on the other side of a dividing social wall in your community or region. Eat where they eat, shop where they shop, and meet people. Listen to their stories. Find out what you have in common. Find out what differences are crucial, and be sensitive to them.

PRAY
FIRST.
PRAY
MOST.

GROUP REVIEW OF WEEK 5

What one truth sticks out from the study this week? What practical changes do you think God is calling you to make based on this week of study?

Look back at the Action Plan for week 5 on page 144. What was the most meaningful and impacting part of that activity for you? Why?

What is the main reason you think we build walls, either physically or metaphorically?

Why is God against walls? What does His resolve to break them down communicate about Him?

What are some walls, both physical and metaphorical, in your life?

What is your "Samaria"? What walls separate you from your Samaria?

What are some other things we can learn about God and His purposes from the story of Saul's conversion and his visit with Ananias?

VIEW DVD MESSAGE
"PRAY FIRST. PRAY MOST."

When the challenge is bigger than you are, you pray _____ ... and you pray _____.

> "While Peter was in prison, the church prayed very earnestly for him" (Acts 12:5, NLT).

Passionate prayers move the heart of God.

There is something about prayer that impacts the direction of _____.

The first fruit of earnest prayer is a good night's _____.

> "Suddenly, there was a bright light in the cell, and an angel of the Lord stood before Peter. The angel struck him on the side to awaken him and said, 'Quick! Get up!' And the chains fell off his wrists. Then the angel told him, 'Get dressed and put on your sandals.' And he did. 'Now put on your coat and follow me,' the angel ordered" (Acts 12:7-8, NLT).

Even the earliest followers of Jesus had trouble believing their prayers really could be _____.

Satan makes it his _____ to interrupt our prayers.

God told us to pray without _____ (1 Thess. 5:17).

Jesus said My house shall be called a house of _____ (Matt. 21:13).

No other spiritual activity is guaranteed the results that prayer is.

"When two of you get together on anything at all on earth and make a prayer of it, my Father in heaven goes into action" (Matt. 18:19, Message).

This session is available for download at *www.lifeway.com/downloads*.

GROUP RESPONSE

How is our attitude toward prayer different than that of the early church? What are some main obstacles to us praying like them?

Why do you think prayer is so important to God?

What does it mean to pray earnestly?

Do you believe you can move the heart of God through prayer? What might keep you from believing it fully?

Why do you think Satan is most effectively countered and battled in prayer?

Day 1
PRAY FIRST. PRAY MOST.

King Herod suffered from a Hitler-level obsession with popularity. He murdered the apostle James to curry favor with the populace. The execution bumped his approval rating, so he jailed Peter and resolved to behead him on the anniversary of Jesus' death. (Would you like a little salt with that wound?)

He placed the apostle under the watchful eye of sixteen Navy Seal sorts and told them, with no tongue in cheek, "He escapes, you die." (Quality control, Herod style.) They bound Peter in chains and secured him three doors deep into the prison.

And what could the church do about it? The problem of an imprisoned Peter stood Goliath-tall over the humble community. They had no recourse: no clout, no political chips to cash. They had nothing but fear-drenched questions. "Who's next? First James, then Peter. Is Herod going to purge the church leadership?"

The church still faces her Goliaths. World hunger. Clergy scandal. Stingy Christians. Corrupt officials. Pea-brained and hard-hearted dictators. Peter in prison is just the first of a long list of challenges too big for the church. So our Jerusalem ancestors left us a strategy. When the problem is bigger than we are—we pray! "But while Peter was in prison, the church prayed very earnestly for him" (Acts 12:5, NLT). They didn't picket the prison, petition the government, protest the arrest, or prepare for Peter's funeral. They prayed. They prayed as if prayer was their only hope, for indeed it was. They prayed "very earnestly for him."

One of our Brazilian church leaders taught me something about earnest prayer. He met Christ during a yearlong stay in a drug-rehab center. His therapy included three one-hour sessions of prayer a day. Patients weren't required to pray, but they were required to attend the prayer meeting. Dozens of recovering drug addicts spent sixty uninterrupted minutes on their knees. I expressed amazement and confessed that my prayers were short and formal. He invited (dared?) me to meet him for prayer. I did the next day. We knelt on the concrete floor of our small church auditorium and began to talk to God. Change that. I talked; he cried, wailed, begged, cajoled, and pleaded. He pounded his fists on the floor, shook a fist toward heaven, confessed, and reconfessed every sin. He recited every promise in the Bible as if God needed a reminder. He prayed like Moses.

When God determined to destroy the Israelites for their golden calf stunt, "Moses begged the Lord his God and said, 'Lord, don't let your anger destroy your people, whom you brought out of Egypt with your great power and strength. Don't let the people of Egypt say, "The Lord brought the Israelites out of Egypt for an evil purpose." … Remember the men who served you— Abraham, Isaac, and Israel. You promised with an oath to them' " (Ex. 32:11-13, NCV).

Moses on Mount Sinai is not calm and quiet, with folded hands and a serene expression. He's on his face one minute, in God's the next. He's on his knees, pointing his finger, lifting his hands. Shedding tears. Shredding his cloak. Wrestling like Jacob at Jabbok for the lives of his people.

And God heard him! "So the Lord changed his mind and did not destroy the people as he had said he might" (v. 14, NCV).

Our passionate prayers move the heart of God. "The effective, fervent prayer of a righteous man avails much" (James 5:16). Prayer does not change God's nature; who He is will never be altered. Prayer does, however, impact the flow of history. God has wired his world for power, but He calls on us to flip the switch.

The Jerusalem church did just that. The church prayed very earnestly for him.

> "The night before Peter was to be placed on trial, he was asleep, fastened with two chains between two soldiers. Others stood guard at the prison gate. Suddenly, there was a bright light in the cell, and an angel of the Lord stood before Peter. The angel struck him on the side to awaken him and said, 'Quick! Get up!' And the chains fell off his wrists. Then the angel told him, 'Get dressed and put on your sandals.' And he did. 'Now put on your coat and follow me,' the angel ordered" (Acts 12:5-8, NLT).

The apostle, who once wondered how Christ could sleep in a storm, now snoozes through his own. Let's give this scene the chuckle it deserves. An angel descends from heaven onto earth. Only God knows how many demons he battled en route. He navigates the Jerusalem streets until he reaches Herod's prison. He passes through three sets of iron doors and a squad of soldiers until he stands in front of Peter. Brightness explodes like a July sun in Death Valley. But Peter sleeps through the wake-up call. The old fisherman dreams of Galilean sea bass.

"Peter."
No response.
"Peter!"
Zzzzz.
"Peter!!!"

Do angels elbow or wing people? Either way, shackles clang on the floor. The angel has to remind groggy Peter how to re-robe. First your sandals. Now your robe. Doors swing open in succession. And somewhere on the avenue to Mary's house, Peter realizes he isn't dreaming. The angel points him in the right direction and departs, muttering something about bringing a trumpet next time.

Rightly stunned, Peter walks to Mary's house. She, at that very hour, is hosting a prayer meeting on his behalf. His friends pack the place and fill the house with earnest intercession.

Peter surely smiles as he hears their prayers. He knocks on the door. The servant answers and, instead of opening it, races back to the prayer circle and announces:

> "Peter is standing at the door!"
> " 'You're out of your mind!' they said. When she insisted, they decided, 'It must be his angel' " (vv. 14-15, NLT).

I confess a sense of relief at that reading. Even the early followers struggled to believe God would hear them. Even when the answer knocked on the door, they hesitated.

We still do. Most of us struggle with prayer. We forget to pray, and when we remember, we hurry through prayers with hollow words. Our minds drift; our thoughts scatter like a covey of quail. Why is this? Prayer requires minimal effort. No location is prescribed. No particular clothing is required. No title or office is stipulated. Yet you'd think we were wrestling a greased pig.

Speaking of pigs, Satan seeks to interrupt our prayers. Our battle with prayer is not entirely our fault. The Devil knows the stories; he witnessed the angel in Peter's cell and the revival in Jerusalem. He knows what happens when we pray. "Our weapons have power from God that can destroy the enemy's strong places" (2 Cor. 10:4, NCV).

Satan is not troubled when Max writes books or prepares sermons, but his knobby knees tremble when Max prays. Satan does not stutter or stumble when you walk through church doors or attend committee meetings. Demons aren't flustered when you read this book. But the walls of hell shake when one person with an honest heart and faithful confession says, "Oh, God, how great thou art."

Satan keeps you and me from prayer. He tries to position himself between us and God. But he scampers like a spooked dog when we move forward. So let's do.

> "Humble yourselves before God. Resist the devil, and he will flee from you. Come close to God, and God will come close to you" (James 4:7-8, NLT).

> "The LORD is close to everyone who prays to him, to all who truly pray to him" (Ps. 145:18, NCV).

When the children of Israel went to battle against the Amalekites, Moses selected the mountain of prayer over the valley of battle (Ex. 17:8-13). The Israelites won.

When Abraham learned about the impending destruction of Sodom and Gomorrah, he "remained standing before the LORD" rather than rush out to warn the cities (Gen. 18:22, NIV).

Advisers informed Nehemiah that Jerusalem was in ruins. He laid a foundation of prayer before he laid a foundation of stone (Neh. 1:4).

Paul's letters contain more requests for prayer than they do appeals for money, possessions, or comforts.

And Jesus. Our prayerful Jesus.

Awaking early to pray (Mark 1:35).
Dismissing people to pray (Matt. 14:23).
Ascending a mountain to pray (Luke 9:28).
Crafting a model prayer to teach us to pray (Matt. 6:9-13).
Cleansing the temple so others could pray (Matt. 21:12-13).
Stepping into a garden to pray (Luke 22:39-46).

Jesus immersed His words and work in prayer. Powerful things happen when we do the same.

Peggy Smith was eighty-four years old. Her sister, Christine, was eighty-two. The years had taken sight from the first and bent the body of the second. Neither could leave their house to attend church. Yet their church needed them. They lived on the Isle of Lewis, off the coast of Scotland. A spiritual darkness had settled upon their village of Barvas. The congregation was losing people, and the youth were mocking the faith, speaking of conversion as a plague. In October 1949 the Presbytery of Free Church called upon their members to pray.

But what could two elderly, housebound sisters do? Quite a lot, they determined. They turned their cottage into an all-night house of prayer. From 10 p.m. to 4 a.m., two nights each week, they asked God to have mercy on their city. After several months Peggy told Christine that God had spoken these words to her: "I will pour water upon him who is thirsty, and floods upon the dry ground."

She was so sure of the message, she urged her pastor to conduct a revival and invite well-known evangelist Duncan Campbell to speak. The pastor did, but Campbell reluctantly declined. Peggy received the news with confidence.

"God hath said he is coming, and he will be here within a fortnight." God changed Campbell's calendar, and within two weeks the meeting began. For five weeks Duncan Campbell preached in Barvas parish. Large crowds gathered in four services at 7 p.m., 10 p.m., midnight, and 3 a.m. The move of God upon the people was undeniable. Hundreds of people were converted. Drinking places closed for lack of patrons. Saloons emptied, and the church grew. The Isle of Lewis tasted the presence of God. All because two women prayed.[1] So:

Let's pray, first. Traveling to help the hungry? Be sure to bathe your mission in prayer. Working to disentangle the knots of injustice? Pray. Weary with a world of racism and division? So is God. And He would love to talk to you about it.

Let's pray, most. Did God call us to preach without ceasing? Or teach without ceasing? Or have committee meetings without ceasing? Or sing without ceasing? No, but He did call us to "pray without ceasing" (1 Thess. 5:17).

Did Jesus declare: My house shall be called a house of study? Fellowship? Music? A house of exposition? A house of activities? No, but He did say, "My house will be called a house of prayer" (Mark 11:17, NIV). No other spiritual activity is guaranteed such results. "When two of you get together on anything at all on earth and make a prayer of it, my Father in heaven goes into action" (Matt. 18:19, Message). He is moved by the humble, prayerful heart.

In late 1964 Communist Simba rebels besieged the town of Bunia in Zaire. They arrested and executed many citizens. A pastor by the name of Zebedayo Idu was one of their victims. They sentenced him to death before a firing squad and placed him in jail for the night. The next morning he and a large number of prisoners were herded onto a truck and driven to a public place for execution. With no explanation the official told the prisoners to line up and number off—"one, two, one, two, one, two." The ones were placed in front of the firing squad. The twos were taken back to the prison. Pastor Zebedayo was among those who were spared.

Back in the jail cell, the prisoners could hear the sound of gunfire. The minister took advantage of the dramatic moment to share the story of Jesus and the hope of heaven. Eight of the prisoners gave their lives to God that day. About the time Pastor Idu finished sharing, an excited messenger came to the door with a release order. The pastor had been arrested by mistake and was free to leave.

He said good-bye to the prisoners and hurried to his home next to the chapel. There he discovered a crowd of believers urgently praying for his release. When they saw the answer to their prayers walk through the door, their prayer service became a praise service.[2] The same God who heard the prayers from Jerusalem heard the prayers from Zaire. He's still listening. Are we still praying?

"Devote yourselves to prayer with an alert mind and a thankful heart. Pray for us, too, that God will give us many opportunities to speak about his mysterious plan concerning Christ." **COLOSSIANS 4:2-3, NLT**

PRAYER

God of Abraham, Isaac, and Jacob, You created all that exists, and You keep it running through Your infinite wisdom and boundless power. Yet You invite me to come to You in prayer, boldly and with the expectation that You will hear me and answer me. Teach me, Lord, to take full advantage of this amazing privilege, especially in regard to reaching others with Your love. Give me a heart for those who have yet to experience the fullness of Your grace, and prompt me to pray for them and for their welfare, both in this world and in eternity. Lord, bring me to the front lines of this battle. In Jesus' name I pray, amen.

Excerpt from Outlive Your Life *(Nashville: Thomas Nelson, 2010), chapter 15.*

THE FIRST RESORT

Oswald Chambers is quoted as saying that prayer isn't preparation for the work; prayer is the work.

How do you feel about that quote? How is prayer the work?

How do we treat it like its preparation for the work?

Far from Chambers's thoughts, we like to use prayer as a bookend for various parts of our days. We pray to begin meetings. Or begin meals. Or as we're falling asleep at night. Or at the occasional football game. It's something we do in order to get ready to do something else.

Even in ministry, we are guilty of making plans and then praying for God to bless them. In all of these examples, prayer becomes something of a formality, almost like an incantation in order to make sure what we want to happen actually comes to pass.

That's a far different opinion about prayer than the church in Acts had. As the book opens, we find that the early church "all continued with one accord in prayer and supplication" (Acts 1:14). Instead of launching out immediately to tackle the world with the gospel, they waited in Jerusalem. And they prayed. After they met initial success on the day of Pentecost and the church counted in the thousands, the explosion of believers troubled the authorities in Jerusalem. They put Peter and John in jail and began to question them. Instead of calling their lawyers or picketing the jail, the early church had a prayer meeting:

"On their release, Peter and John went back to their own people and reported all the chief priests and elders had said to them. When they heard this, they raised their voices in prayer to God. ...

"After they prayed, the place where they were meeting was shaken. And they were filled with the Holy Spirit and spoke the word of God boldly" (Acts 4:23-31, NIV).

Then, in Acts 6, when an oversight caused threat of division, the church leadership assigned trustworthy men to distribute food to the widows so they could spend their time in prayer and teaching the word (see Acts 6:3-5).

Nothing could keep the leaders from prayer, for they understood that prayer was an absolute necessity. Prayer empowered, fueled, and emboldened them. We think prayer is a good idea but not a driving force. Not an essential tool. Not oxygen for our spiritual lungs. Not our "first" resort.

What comes to your mind when you think of prayer?

How do you think God feels about your prayer life?

PRAY FERVENTLY

So when Peter landed in prison once again, the believing community knew what to do.

Read Acts 12:1-5. What was the response of the church when Peter was imprisoned?

If the same thing happened in this country today, how would the church respond?

The church prayed. That's it. They gathered together and approached the throne of grace. Doesn't it seem like they should have done something more? Their leader was jailed. Their future was insecure. The problem before them was enormous. And yet all they could think to do was pray. We might be tempted to look at this as the actions (or inactions) of cowards. They should be acting, not "just praying."

But perhaps the Jerusalem church, even in their brief existence, had become convinced of a fact that still exists in the realm of doubt for us: Passionate prayers move the heart of God.

Read James 5:16. What do you think it means to pray "fervently"?

Is that how you would describe your prayer life? What is one word you would use to describe it?

Prayer has power to change things, both inside and outside of us. Sometimes fervently praying changes the actual circumstances we are praying about. But we can count on the fact that praying is always going to change our attitudes, preferences, and level of patience. We should not hesitate in exercising our God-given privilege to approach Him. He wants us to. He wants to be moved. He wants to see things change. And He has chosen for prayer to be the vehicle on which that change rides.

PRAY WITHOUT CEASING

Let's pray as the Jerusalem church did. Let's pray first. But also, let's pray most.

> **Read 1 Thessalonians 5:17. What do you think it means to pray without ceasing? Have you ever tried to do so? What was the experience like?**

God wants us to be so committed to prayer that our internal monologue becomes a dialogue. We begin to have ceaseless conversation with Him about our kids. About the events on the world news. About our coworker in the next cubicle. About the big decisions we have to make. He wants us to talk to Him, and then listen for His response.

When we pray, things happen. Indeed, no spiritual activity is guaranteed the results of prayer.

God is not moved by men of standing but by men of kneeling. He is today, and He was when the church approached the throne of grace on behalf of their jailed leader.

PRAYER

Thank You, ever-attentive God, for never slumbering or sleeping. Thank You for opening the lines of communication. Forgive us for treating prayer as an add-on to the rest of our lives. Teach us the power of prayer today. In Jesus' name I pray, amen.

EARNEST PRAYER

Peter was imprisoned. He was locked and guarded behind three impenetrable doors. No way in, and no way out.

The church saw this as a moment for prayer. But they didn't just pray As the New Living Translation says, they prayed "very earnestly for him" (Acts 12:5).

> **What's the difference between praying and praying earnestly?**

> **What does an earnest prayer sound like? What does someone who is praying earnestly look like?**

There are certain qualities that mark earnest prayer, separating it from the casual conversations we often attempt to have with God. First of all, earnest prayer is nothing if not honest.

HONEST PRAYER

Not pretty. Not polished. Certainly not formal. But honest. Why are our prayers so often flooded with pretense and flowery words? We use language like that with another human being when we are nervous about coming to the point. But that approach doesn't make sense with God. For the simple truth is that He already knows.

> **How might your prayers sound different if you resolved to be completely honest with God?**

God is the great heart-searcher. He's the great mind reader. He looks deeply within us and knows what we are really feeling and thinking. In fact, He knows us better than we know ourselves.

No matter what we say in prayer, God will never be dismayed or surprised. In fact, absolute honesty in prayer is an expression of faith in the God who loves us anyway.

PERSISTENT PRAYER

Earnest prayer is not only honest prayer. It's also persistent prayer.

> **Would you be nervous or excited if someone told you to pray for an hour? Why?**

The persistent nature of earnest prayer is vividly illustrated by a story Jesus told about a woman seeking justice.

> **Read this parable in Luke 18:1-5. What do you picture in your mind when you think about this widow?**

> **Was Jesus teaching that we can wear God down with persistency? If not, then what was His point?**

There she is again, the judge thought to himself. Didn't she ever sleep? Every day, here was this woman. Waiting outside his chambers. Standing in the gallery. Calling on the phone. Making appointment after appointment with his secretary. She never quits. This judge, even though he had little invested in this woman's case and cared little about her complaint, finally decided that it wasn't worth his time. Her earnestness—her persistence—wore him out. And justice was hers.

Jesus meant to encourage us to keep praying. Keep asking. Keep approaching. But He wasn't encouraging us to do it in order to wear God out, that somehow by our stubbornness we can outlast the Almighty. He meant in this parable to say that if a judge who has no moral certitude and little concern for justice can be moved into action by persistence, how much more willing to help us is our Father in heaven?

DESPERATE PRAYER

The earnest prayer is honest. And it's persistent. But there's also something else that characterizes the earnest prayer: desperation. The church of Acts 12 had no other option but to pray. They had no political clout. No chips to cash. No favors to pull in. They were, in short, in a desperate situation. That desperation fueled fervent prayer.

What is one time when you have prayed desperately?

How was that prayer different than some of your other experiences in prayer?

One of the reasons we don't pray earnestly is that we fail to grasp just how urgent the situations are around us. Yet if we zoomed out, we would see the problems facing the church are no smaller than the ones that spawned such earnest prayer in the first century.

With the multitude of orphans, homelessness, disease, and spiritual apathy in the world today, if there was ever a time for desperation, this is it. But most of us are too insulated to realize it.

We spend much of our lives trying to protect ourselves from desperation. We have deep freezes to store food. We have insurance policies against catastrophic events. We have home warranties just in case. That's also why we turn the station when the hungry children commercial comes on. It's why we refuse to go to the doctor when the symptoms persist. It's why we avoid difficult conversations with family members. We will do anything possible to deny the truth of our desperateness.

Ironically, our desperation is a key ingredient to moving the heart of God. The old adage says, "God helps those who help themselves." That is a radically unbiblical concept. God doesn't help those who help themselves; God helps those who know they cannot help themselves.

Why might God choose to involve Himself particularly with those who know they cannot help themselves?

His commitment to the widow and the orphan, His concern for the poor, and His identification with the hungry and the weary traveler tell us that God loves to be near and help the desperate.

We could all use a little more honesty, persistence, and desperation in our prayer lives. When we look at the world, we have many things to be honest, persistent, and desperate about. So go to God. He's ready. He knows you're coming. He doesn't grow tired of hearing you.

And He will spring into action, moved by the cries of His people.

PRAYER

We confess, Father, that when we pray, we don't really do so earnestly. Help us to see how much we truly need You and how ready You are to deliver. Open our eyes to these realities, we pray. In Jesus' name I pray, amen.

PEACEFUL SLEEP

Seems like a great occasion for restlessness. You had just seen one of your friends executed. The same egomaniac responsible for his death has you under lock and key. And guards upon guards. Tomorrow is your "trial"—more likely your sentencing, too. So how do you choose to spend the night? Pacing back and forth? Playing over potential scenarios? Writing letters to cherished friends and family?

If you were Peter, you'd be sleeping. Very well.

Why do you think Peter was able to sleep so soundly in this circumstance?

What does his state of mind reveal about his beliefs?

According to Acts 12, Peter was so sound asleep that his liberating angel had some difficulty in waking him up. But after a miraculous jailbreak and short trip to Mary's house, Peter found his friends praying fervently for his release.

But despite their fervent prayers, there is a realistic picture of the Jerusalem church painted here. Though they no doubt prayed for the miraculous, they had trouble believing when the miraculous actually happened.

Read Acts 12:11-16. What, in these verses, can you relate to based on your own experience in prayer?

Are you ever frustrated by your prayer life? If you could change one thing immediately about your prayer life, what would it be?

Prayer moves the heart of God, but something else happens when we pray. The Devil gets angry.

What is it that troubles Satan about prayer?

When we toss up haphazard prayers before dinner or a civic meeting, chances are we aren't thinking of prayer in its proper context. To think of prayer rightly, we must realize that all of life is war. As John Piper puts it, "Many of our problems with prayer and much of our weakness in prayer come from the fact that we are not all on active duty, and yet we still try to use the transmitter. We have taken a wartime walkie-talkie and tried to turn it into a civilian intercom to call the servants for another cushion in the den."[3]

Take a moment and analyze the dimensions of your prayer life. What do you pray for most often? Least often?

Why do you think we pray so often for things that would make us more comfortable?

BATTLING IN PRAYER

If we did the above exercise, we would probably be shocked to read the text of our prayers. Sure, there are some items thrown in there for other people and maybe a mention or two of the world at large, but there is very little that would qualify as battle language. Most of our prayers, in fact, are more like appeals to a rich grandfather for a bigger piece of the material pie.

That kind of praying fails to realize our conflict with evil. In such a conflict, our weapon is prayer. The battle is fought on our knees.

Prayer is a wartime walkie-talkie. It's our source for the reinforcements and supplies we need. It's our means of communication with headquarters. It's our lifeline, not something to be used for material comforts.

Are you comfortable with this description of prayer? Why or why not?

Read Ephesians 6:10-12. In what sense are we in a battle? How aware are you of that battle?

We should do all we are able to alleviate the physical suffering of others. We must free slaves. We must tackle oppression. We must confront injustice. But we must realize that behind each of these physical realities are spiritual strongholds, and it's there where the deeper battle lies. We must pray, for prayer is the only way we can attack the second—and higher—level of reality at work. Prayer is the only way the true strongholds will fall.

What are three practical ways you need to change your mode of praying in order to begin to see it as battle?

How can you become more aware of these strongholds in the world that need to be attacked in prayer?

Sound daunting? I hope so. It's staggering to think that when we fall to our knees in prayer we enter a battle that is already waging all around us. Yet this is precisely what happens. The greatest spiritual victories in the universe aren't won in the open but behind closed doors.

The greatest warriors for the kingdom of God are often the least visible, those that do their fighting from their knees.

PRAYER

We need to get in the fight, Father. For too long we have sat on the sidelines. Help us to engage. To fight. To see our time on our knees as universally important. And thank You that in this, too, You make up for what we lack. We trust even now in Jesus who intercedes on our behalf. In Jesus' name I pray, amen.

STILL LISTENING

The same God who heard the prayers from Jerusalem is still listening to the prayers of His people today. Most of us can recall something happening that we would have thought impossible, and yet it came to pass specifically because the people of God prayed.

> **What are the most significant things you have seen happen as a result of prayer? Did those events have any lasting effect on your prayer life?**

Problem is that for every story of a miracle there is an equally powerful story of the deliverance that did not come. The Christ follower who was cut down. The miraculous that didn't happen. The tears of pain rather than of joy. We live in a day and time when more Christians have been martyred for the faith than ever before. What happens when you pray—earnestly, honestly, and desperately—and yet it seems as though the prayers bounce off of the ceiling and come right back down?

OPPOSITION IS INEVITABLE

Whether it's political, societal, or familial, there always have been and always will be those seeking to put down the Christian faith. We all face opposition.

Peter did. He landed in jail. The church did. They landed on their knees. But I have to wonder about the subject of the prayers in Acts 12. What did they beseech the Lord for? What exactly did they pray?

**What specifically do you think the church prayed for?
What makes you say that?**

**Do you think deliverance was their primary objective?
Why or why not?**

When bad things start happening, the prayers start going up. And more times than not, those prayers are for relief. For comfort. For deliverance. But given their past history, I tend to think that maybe the prayer meeting when Peter was in jail had a different focus.

See, Acts 12 wasn't the first time Peter found himself in prison.

Read about his first arrest in Acts 4:1-22. Why were Peter and John arrested?

How did they respond to their arrest?

Upon their arrest, the ruling authorities demanded an explanation for their insurrection. Those same authorities were the ones who, not so long ago, publicly executed their leader. Now His message continued to spread.

They demanded an explanation, and Peter gave it to them. He didn't back down in his words. Apparently a night in jail didn't cool Peter's heels. It only heated his resolve: "There is no other name under heaven given among men by which we must be saved" (Acts 4:12).

That's pretty definite. No wiggle room there. But there was nothing the authorities could do; Peter and John were leading a movement that was gaining momentum. Further action might incite an all-out riot. So they released them under strict orders to keep their mouths shut.

Peter and John went back to their fellowship and reported the happenings. Acts 4:24 records that they all raised their voices unanimously to pray. But what? What would they ask for?

> **What do you expect the crux of the believers' prayer to be at this moment?**

> **Read Acts 4:24-31. What did they pray for? Does that surprise you? Why or why not?**

WHAT THEY DIDN'T ASK FOR

Shocking. Astounding. So far removed from what we would pray were we in their situation. The church began their prayer with praise. They called to mind the immense power of God, that He is the Ruler of the entire universe, the One in control of all. This was their God—not a pathetic idol or a powerless deity. Their God was the Maker of heaven, earth, and everything in them. A host of angels at His disposal. With the flick of a finger He could remove those priests from power.

So what would they ask this God? What mighty work did they request?

I suppose I'm not nearly as shocked by what they asked for as what they didn't ask for. A heart attack for Caiaphas? Nope. Religious liberty in the Roman Empire? Don't think so. Angelic protection for their leaders? Not that either. They asked not for deliverance but for boldness to proclaim the message of Jesus Christ.

With the power of God at their disposal, they chose to ask for even greater courage. They didn't ask for an end to the opposition; they asked for boldness in the face of opposition.

> **Why would they have done that? What does their prayer reveal about their priorities?**

> **Why was the persecution a chance for the gospel to be advanced?**

When beseeching the great God of all, the One standing at the edge of heaven ready to spring into action, they asked for boldness. And I think God smiled at that request. For in their prayer, the early church revealed their firm belief that some things are more important.

More important than safety. More important than health. More important than comfort. Some things are simply more important.

Not deliverance. Boldness. And when they were done praying, the room started shaking. God answered.

> **Can you think of a circumstance when bad circumstances have fueled the gospel?**

> **Why is the testimony of someone in the worst of circumstances more meaningful than someone in the best of circumstances?**

What if we stopped focusing on our circumstances and started praying for boldness? What if we were more concerned about the gospel than we were about our own comfort? We would be shocked at how quickly things would start changing.

Friends, through the power of God, the world can change. So what can we do today that will be worthy of mention in heaven? What can we do today to outlive our lives?

For heaven's sake, let's get busy.

PRAYER

You have charged us, God, with changing the world. We recognize the power You have given to us in the Holy Spirit. We see the resources at our disposal. Now help us to do something about it. Give us vision, courage, and boldness as we seek to outlive our lives for Your sake. In Jesus' name I pray, amen.

OUTLIVING YOUR LIFE THIS WEEK

Scripture Memory: "Devote yourselves to prayer with an alert mind and a thankful heart. Pray for us, too, that God will give us many opportunities to speak about his mysterious plan concerning Christ" (Col. 4:2-3, NLT).

Action Plan: Create a personal action plan with the goal of outliving your life. Determine how your gifts, passion, and opportunities best fit into God's plan to serve your neighborhood, community, and world. Overlay that template on your personal calendar to put it into action.

ENDNOTES

WEEK 1

1. UNICEF, "The State of the World's Children 2009: Maternal and Newborn Health," [online, cited 17 May 2010]. Available from the Internet: *www.unicef. org/sowc09/report/report.php.*

2. Food and Agriculture Organization of the United Nations, *The State of Food Insecurity in the World: Economic Crises—Impacts and Lessons Learned* [online, cited 17 May 2010]. Available from the Internet: *ftp://ftp.fao.org/docrep/ fao/012/i0876e/i0876e.pdf.*

3. UNICEF, "The State of the World's Children 2007: Women and Children; The Double Dividend of Gender Equality," [online, cited 17 May 2010]. Available from the Internet: *www.unicef.org/sowc07/docs/sowc07.pdf.*

4. Anup Shah, "Today, Over 24,000 Children Died Around the World," Global Issues, [online], 28 March 2010 [cited 17 May 2010]. Available from the Internet:*www. globalissues.org/article/715/today-over-24000-children-died-around-the-world*

5. Peter Greer and Phil Smith, *The Poor Will Be Glad: Joining the Revolution to Lift the World out of Poverty* (Grand Rapids: Zondervan, 2009), 26.

6. Ronald J. Sider, *Rich Christians in an Age of Hunger: Moving from Affluence to Generosity* (Nashville: Thomas Nelson, 2005), 10.

7. Ibid., 35.

8. UNICEF, "The State of the World's Children 2009," 133.

9. The percentage of Christians in the United States is 76.8 percent, and the population of the United States in 2009 was approximately 307,212, 000, according to the CIA, *The World Factbook 2009* [online, cited 17 May 2010]. Available from the Internet: *https://www.cia.gov/library/publications/the-world-factbook.*

10. UNAIDS and World Health Organization, "AIDS Epidemic Update: November 2009," [online, cited 24 May 2010]. Available from the Internet: *http://data. unaids.org/pub/Report/2009/JC1700_Epi_Update_2009_en.pdf.*

WEEK 2

1. Hilary Le Cornu with Joseph Shulam, *A Commentary on the Jewish Roots of Acts* (Jerusalem: Netivyah Bible Instruction Ministry, 2003), 144.

2. Alfred Edersheim, *The Life and Times of Jesus the Messiah,* (Peabody, MA: Hendrickson Publishers, Inc., 1993), 81-2.

3. M. Paul Lewis, ed., *Ethnologue: Languages of the World,* 16th ed. (Dallas: SIL International, 2009), [online, cited 17 May 2010]. Available from the Internet: *www.ethnologue.com.*

4. If you want to explore in detail your "you-niqueness" and how to discern it, see my book *Cure for the Common Life: Living in Your Sweet Spot* (Nashville: Thomas Nelson, 2005).

5. Telephone interview with Jo Anne Lyon, conducted by David Drury, 23 June 2009.

WEEK 4

1. Richard Stearns, *The Hole in Our Gospel* (Nashville: Thomas Nelson, 2008), 11.

2. *The Expositor's Bible Commentary with the New International Version of the Holy Bible* (Grand Rapids: Zondervan, 1990), 2:633–35.

3. Walter Bruggeman, "Isaiah and the Mission of the Church," (sermon, Mars Hill Bible Church, Grand Rapids, MI, 13 July 2009).

4. United Nations Development Programme, "Fighting Climate Change: Human Solidarity in a Divided World," Human Development Report 2007/2008 [online, cited 17 May 2010]. Available from the Internet: *http://hdr.undp.org/en/reports/global/hdr2007-2008/*.

5. "Closer to the Music," *U2.com* [online], 30 July 2009 [cited 17 May 2010]. Available from the Internet: *www.u2.com/news/article/682.*

6. United Nations World Food Programme, "WFP Facts Blast," [online], December 2009 [cited 17 May 2010]. Available from the Internet: *http://home.wfp.org/stellent/groups/public/documents/communications/wfp187701.pdf.*

7. Anup Shah, "Today, Over 24,000 Children Died Around the World," Global Issues, [online], 28 March 2010 [cited 17 May 2010]. Available from the Internet: *www.globalissues.org/article/715/today-over-24000-children-died-around-the-world*

WEEK 5

1. Rick Reilly, "There Are Some Games in Which Cheering for the Other Side Feels Better Than Winning," *ESPN: The Magazine* [online, cited 24 May 2010]. Available from the Internet: *http://sports.espn.go.com/espnmag/story?section=magazine&id=3789373.*

2. Hilary Le Cornu with Joseph Shulam, *A Commentary on the Jewish Roots of Acts* (Jerusalem: Netivyah Bible Instruction Ministry, 2003), 403.

WEEK 6

1. Oliver W. Price, "Needed: A Few Committed People to Pray for Revival," Bible Prayer Fellowship, [online, cited 17 May 2010]. Available from the Internet: *www.praywithchrist.org/prayer/committed.php.*

2. R. Kent Hughes, ed., *Acts: The Church Afire* (Wheaton, IL: Crossway Books, 1996), 169-70.

3. John Piper, *Desiring God* (Sisters, OR: Multnomah Publishers, Inc., 2003), 177.